Who Is This Man — This Jesus?

Fifteen Dramatic
Lenten Monologues

Richard A. Eddy

CSS Publishing Company, Inc., Lima, Ohio

WHO IS THIS MAN — THIS JESUS?

WHO IS THIS MAN — THIS JESUS?

Copyright © 2009 by
CSS Publishing Company, Inc.
Lima, Ohio

The original purchaser may photocopy material in this publication for use as it was intended (worship material for worship use; educational material for classroom use; dramatic material for staging or production). No additional permission is required from the publisher for such copying by the original purchaser only. Inquiries should be addressed to: Permissions, CSS Publishing Company, Inc., 517 South Main Street, Lima, Ohio 45804.

Scripture quotations are from the New Revised Standard Version of the Bible, copyright 1989 by the Division of Christian Education of the National Council of the Churches of Christ in the USA. Used by permission.

For more information about CSS Publishing Company resources, visit our website at www.csspub.com or email us at csr@csspub.com or call (800) 241-4056.

Cover design by Barbara Spencer
ISBN-13: 978-0-7880-2600-3
ISBN-10: 0-7880-2600-3

PRINTED IN USA

To my wife, Karen, for her ideas,
encouragement, and feedback,
but mostly for her unwavering faith
as a true "woman of the promise."

Table Of Contents

Who Is This Man?

A Soldier Of King Herod

(He looks around as he comes in, as if looking for someone, then fixes on one person and calls loudly.)

Hey, you there! I have a question for you, and there might be a shekel or two in it for you if you tell me truthfully! *(shakes bag of coins temptingly)* I am looking for someone; perhaps you can tell me where I might find him. What name? Do you mean my name or his? His? Well, that's the problem; I don't know his name. *(quickly)* No, wait, don't leave — I know some things about him that may help you to know who I'm seeking; you see, there were some, how should I put it, some unusual circumstances surrounding his birth.

He was born not far from here, over in Bethlehem, some thirty years ago — back in the days when Caesar Augustus was ruler of Rome, and Herod was king over Judea. At least in those days, we had our own king, not a Roman governor like we do now. I know, Herod was a cruel ruler, and half Gentile, but that means he was half Jewish, too *(sarcastically)*, not like his excellency, Mr. Roman Pontius Pilate! How do I know so much about King Herod? I was one of his soldiers.

(suddenly sad, looks down) It is because I was Herod's soldier that I seek this nameless man today. You see, I was stationed in Herod's court, one of the many bodyguards to protect him from all the assassins he constantly feared, but who never came. One day, as I stood guard near Herod's throne, we received a strange delegation of foreigners. From their clothing and turbans I made them out to be Chaldeans — that class of wise men and stargazers we call magi. And when they spoke, well, their speech, though highly educated, was definitely heavy with Eastern accents.

I assumed these magi had come to pay their respects to Herod, and perhaps to offer a gift from their own king or to ask for protection for their caravan. But instead of the usual greetings and pleasantries that other visitors offer to the king *(mocks their fawning)*: "O King, live forever! You are like a tree that spreads out its branches to provide blessings for the people under your rule! All the birds of the nations come to rest in your branches! The nations

9

salute your wisdom!" Instead of all that, the magi got right to the point of their visit. They asked, "Where is the child who has been born king of the Jews? For we observed his star at its rising, and have come to pay him homage."

Herod was eating a fig right then, and for a moment, I thought he was going to choke on it! He coughed it up, and used that moment to regain his composure, though for a second I could see anger and hatred flash in his eyes. My mouth dried up, for I feared that he would order me to kill these men for suggesting there could possibly be another king of the Jews beside Herod! He had already killed others, even members of his own family, for less an offense than that! But to my surprise, Herod recovered and with a forced smile, he called in his religious scholars and advisors to see what they might say.

While the advisors consulted their scrolls, word of the magi's request spread like wildfire through the palace and out onto the streets. Everyone was upset by the news. Those who knew Herod the best held their breaths, waiting for his wrath to strike out, but to our amazement, he kept smiling, and waited for the scholars to make their report, though he laid off the figs for the rest of the day.

Soon the scholars came in with their research. They reported that long ago the prophet Micah had prophesied where the king would be born. We were astounded to hear them read, "But you, O Bethlehem of Ephrathah, who are one of the little clans of Judah, from you shall come forth for me one who is to rule in Israel, whose origin is from of old, from ancient days" (Micah 5:2). So, not only was there a prophecy, the birthplace was close at hand, maybe six or seven miles from the palace!

Herod dismissed the advisors with a wave of his hand, and called the magi closer to him. He spoke quietly, so not everyone would hear, but I was close enough to make out most of what he said. He asked them when exactly the star had first appeared. I couldn't make out their whispered answer (thanks to their accents!), but I could make out what Herod said next. He sent them to Bethlehem, saying, "Go and search diligently for the child; and when you have found him, bring me word so that I may also go and pay him homage."

When I heard him say that ... well, it's a good thing I wasn't eating any figs myself! I knew Herod would *never* pay homage to anyone else, or even allow any challenger to his throne to live. He maintained his smile until the magi departed, but not one second more! His face changed and turned ugly; he began shouting orders, and called us soldiers to his side. His orders to me were simple, "Tomorrow, when the magi return with the exact location of this so-called 'King of the Jews,' you will proceed with a detachment of troops and bring his body to me."

That night I slept fitfully for a few hours, then got up and stepped outside to clear my head. Why did I have to be on duty that day, to be picked to slay some helpless infant boy? What had the boy done, except be born in Bethlehem? Who was this man-child, that a king would fear him and issue his death warrant? I pondered these questions without answers, and prayed that I would not have to deliver the spear stroke myself. Then I remembered the star. I turned toward the southwestern sky, in the direction of Bethlehem — and my heart skipped a beat, for there it was! One star, brighter than all the rest, brighter than I ever remembered seeing, clearly marking the way to that city of David. Could this really be fulfillment of prophecy?

Morning came and with it, my sense of dread. We expected the magi to return in the morning, but when noon came and went without them, Herod became more and more agitated. Finally, midafternoon came and when it became clear the magi were not coming back, Herod exploded with rage. He ordered us to march to Bethlehem and carry out the execution. But I was confused, so I bowed before Herod and asked, "But your majesty, how will you know which boy it is without the wise men to tell us?" Herod's answer chilled me to my bones: "I don't care which one he is! If you kill *all* the boys age two and younger, then you're sure to get him, too. Kill them; kill them all!"

Now, I was a soldier. I had done my share of fighting and killing, but that was against rebels and armed robbers attacking caravans. How could I be asked to kill an innocent boy, let alone all the male infants of Bethlehem? I started to open my mouth in protest, but Herod looked at me with such a look, that I shut my mouth without another word except, "Yes, sire."

I don't want to talk about what we did in Bethlehem, except to say that I was so ashamed of it that I quit the king's guard soon afterward, right after Herod himself died. Too bad for those boys that Herod didn't die first! The burden of guilt I have carried for these thirty years has tormented me — at times I wish I had refused the orders and been executed myself, rather than be haunted by my memories all this time. If only there were some way to get rid of my guilt, to find forgiveness. If only I could go back and change what I did, to ask forgiveness of those families and of God.

That day in Bethlehem, some people claimed they had seen the Magi go to a certain house, and then the family who lived there disappeared. I thought they were making it up — trying to save their own sons by sending us on a wild ostrich chase. But over the years, I've never been able to shake the thought that possibly, just possibly, the boy — the King of the Jews — survived.

Now I hear that there is a man going about proclaiming the kingdom of God is near. People say miracles follow wherever he goes and that he preaches forgiveness of sins through repentance and baptism. Some have even begun to call him ... a king! He's about the right age, a little over thirty. The only problem: He is said to be from Nazareth, not Bethlehem, but if his family fled from Bethlehem when he was an infant, they could have gone anywhere from there, including Nazareth!

Please, tell me! Who is this man from Nazareth, and where is he now? I must find him, I must know if he is the one born King of the Jews. I must know if I can finally find forgiveness for what I did!

This is why you must help me, if you can. *(Take out a coin, then two, then dump the whole bag as if the money means nothing compared to the answer it might purchase.)* Here, take some money; take what you want, only tell me: Is the one I was sent to kill, still alive? For thirty years I have prayed that he is. Now may the Lord grant this old soldier one last request! Let me see him once before I die!

12

The Centurion Of Capernaum

(Wearing a centurion's uniform, he is seated at a desk on which are papers, helmet, an hourglass, and an unlit candle. One paper is in hand, which he is reading carefully. After a few seconds of reading, he stands, sets the paper down and speaks with authority as he calls to various officials.)

Marcus! Take word to the men — we muster in the square in one hour — full battle dress and weapons! All except the third century — they remain for garrison duty.

Gracus! Tell the quartermaster — rations for one week for the cohort — ready to go within the hour!

Lucius! It seems, good Lucius, that we have some work ahead of us — we've been summoned to join the legion at Tiberias. Another self-appointed messiah has attacked one of our patrols and the procurator wants us to stamp out this rebellion quickly. Assemble the centurions at once! And send a rider to the Fortress of Antonia in Jerusalem with this reply *(says with weight)*: "As you have commanded, so it has been done." *(picks up helmet as if to leave with it when he "sees" another aide approaching)*

Yes, Quintus, what is it? Some visitors to see me? This is not a good time! I must prepare for the departure of the cohort *(dismissive gesture)*; perhaps these visitors can come back next month. What do they want, anyway? *(listens, then shows sudden interest)* Oh, *him*? Well *(picks up the hourglass)*, if it's about *him*, maybe I can spare a *few* minutes. *(turns hourglass over and sets it and the helmet down)* Send them in! *(slight pause as the audience "enters")*

(straightens up, brings arm across chest in salute) Greetings. I am Decimus Flavius, commanding centurion of the Fifth Cohort, Sixth Iron Legion of the Senate and People of Rome, and garrison commander here in Capernaum of Galilee. My aide tells me that you have come to inquire as to the location of a certain Jesus of Nazareth. Is this true? *(nods head in agreement with them)*

You look eager to see him; you are followers, perhaps? Yes? Sorry, I wish could help you, but I don't know where he is right now. One persistent rumor says he and his disciples were seen on the road south toward Jericho; another says he is in Jerusalem. All I know for certain is, he is no longer in Capernaum, though he was here not too long ago. I know he was here because I saw him, and because, well, because I saw what he did: a miracle that saved my own servant's life.

Oh, you hadn't heard about that? Well, it was amazing to see, though I had no doubt Jesus could actually do it. Still, that he would so bless me and my servant who are not his people! If I can't tell you where to find Jesus, I can at least praise him by telling you what he did. Sit, and I will tell you the story.

First, a little background. Though I am a Roman centurion, I'm not the normal Roman soldier. Most of my men are very religious, after a fashion. They believe in the traditional Roman gods and goddesses, and they take on the local gods wherever they are stationed, just in case. Except here in Palestine — they don't care for the Jewish God. His commandments not to kill, steal, or commit adultery just don't fit the way they live. Not to mention, the Jewish God is jealous and won't allow the worship of any other god except him. Not good for a soldier who's trying to keep all the gods happy. Also, the men are very superstitious; they want something they can hold in their hands or tuck into their tunics for protection in a battle, so they don't have much use for an invisible God who doesn't allow any images of himself.

I was not one for religion or superstitious ways. My god has been Rome and its legions; my worship is fighting and taking care of the men assigned to my command. However, I have come to realize there is something to the Jewish God. They regard him so holy they don't even call him by name — just his titles of Lord, or God — but he claims to be the only God there is, unlike all the idols and superstitions of the nations. This God is certainly different; he calls us to holiness, like himself. He claims power over all the earth. And he promises to send a Savior, called the Christ or the Messiah, to save his people, and all nations, from their sins.

Are you surprised that I know the Jewish Messiah? After arresting several phony messiahs to keep the peace around here, I went to the local rabbis to learn who and what the Messiah was supposed to be. They told me about the prophecies, and said they expected him to come at any time. I wanted to know more, so I began attending some services at the local synagogue and listened to the rabbis teach from their scriptures. I was moved by what I heard, and before long I was a regular attendee, and yes, even a worshiper, drawn to this invisible God who had created the world by his voice of command. He spoke and it was obeyed *(with weight)* "As you have commanded, so it has been done." I like that in a god.

I continued to worship and support the synagogue. I became friendly with the elders, though they would never come under the roof of my house, since I am after all, still a Gentile. Then, when the old synagogue burned down and they needed to build a new one, I stepped forward with money, materials, and the strong backs of some of my soldiers who, shall we say, owed some community service to the locals to make up for some recent brutish behavior.

(becomes more serious) Not long after that, my personal servant, Demetrius, fell ill. He who had always served me well, whom I had come to love as my own brother, lay sick on what I feared would be his deathbed. My servant was ill and nothing the physicians did was helping. He just became worse and worse. Frustrated, I called the physicians to me and commanded them, "Heal my servant!" as if they were foot soldiers marching to battle. They protested that they had done everything they could, but I commanded them to do more! They somberly shook their heads and whispered that the end was near.

I couldn't accept that Demetrius was dying, so I sent for the Jewish elders, to seek their prayers; perhaps the God who had created everything by his command could heal one little person. They arrived in a few moments, offering both condolences to me and prayers for Demetrius. Then one of them asked if I had heard of a prophet and healer named Jesus of Nazareth. I had not, so the elder explained that this Jesus was traveling around Galilee preaching remarkable things about God's kingdom, and was healing all kinds of illnesses, casting out demons, restoring hearing and sight, and some say, even raising the dead! Not only that, this Jesus had just arrived right here in Capernaum!

When I heard that, my heart skipped and I knew we had to find Jesus and bring him to heal my servant. I told the elders to go find him and bring him to me immediately. They took off at a run, and I paced around wondering if this Jesus would make it in time.

I'm so used to giving orders, why couldn't I make it all turn out the way I wanted? Why couldn't I just give a command and have Jesus appear right here, right now? Why couldn't I just command Demetrius to be healed and get out of bed? Why couldn't I...? That was when it hit me: If Jesus has God's power to heal Demetrius, he didn't have to even come here to do it! Like it is with me, I can give a command, and soldiers obey me even at a distance. Certainly Jesus can do the same! All he has to do is speak the word, and then, "As you have commanded, so it has been done."

I spoke quickly to a couple friends who were standing helplessly nearby. I told them to catch up with the elders, find Jesus, and give him this new message: "Lord, I am not worthy to have you come under my roof; but only speak the word, and my servant will be healed. For I also am a man under authority, with soldiers under me; and I say to one, 'Go,' and he goes, and to another, 'Come,' and he comes, and to my slave, 'Do this,' and the slave does it."

My friends took off and I settled down in a chair beside my dying servant. Would the elders and my friends find Jesus in time? Would he even want to heal a Gentile who is servant to a Roman officer? I had the military might and authority of the Roman empire at my command, but all I could do was sit helplessly and wait.

When I heard my name being called, I thought it was a friend returning with word from Jesus. But the doorway was empty, and the only one left in the room with me was poor Demetrius. I hung my head again and prayed as I had learned in the synagogue, when I heard my name again, stronger and louder this time. I looked up and saw it was Demetrius! He sat up and swung his feet off the side of the bed and stretched as if he had just taken a nap! He asked what was happening and why I was just staring at him. He smiled and said, "Sir, I've never seen you at such a loss for words!"

I wasn't at a loss for long! I told him everything, even as I'm telling you now. We rejoiced together over the healing, and when my friends returned, I ran to the door to tell them the good news. They, too, rejoiced, and told me what Jesus said to them when they gave him my message: "Truly I tell you, in no one in Israel have I found such faith."

Who is this man, this Jesus? Who is this man who can heal a dying servant from a distance, who has God's authority over nature and people? Who is this man who has compassion even for an enemy soldier who occupies his country? Could this be the man the rabbis teach about in the synagogue? In a land of many false messiahs, could Jesus be the real Christ they — and we — have been waiting for? I hope he is; no, I should say, I *know* he is, for I have found him.

And now, may you find him, too. But you'll have to do that on your own *(takes up helmet)*, because I am a man under authority, and I have orders to obey. *(salutes again)*

(pauses on the way out) May the true God go with you in your journey!

Malchus, Servant Of Caiaphas

(He comes hurrying in, looking back over his shoulder as if he's being followed. He keeps putting his hands over his right ear, feeling it as if to make sure it's still there. His costume includes a dagger in his cloak. He looks back once more while asking his first question.)

Who *is* this man? *(looks to audience)* How is this possible? Look at my ear, will you? *(turns head to show right ear to everyone)* Can you see it? Do you see what's wrong with it? Do you? That's right! Nothing's wrong with it! And that's what I'm saying, "How is it possible that nothing's wrong with it?" You know why I'm asking that question: I'll tell you why! Just a half hour ago, that ear wasn't there! No, I'm not joking; my ear had been cut off and was lying on the ground, and I had a hole in the side of my head where my ear used to be. Then, *he* picked up my ear and put it back in place, and suddenly, it was all healed up as if nothing had ever happened!

Yes, I know it's not possible! *(feels the ear with one hand, hardly believing that it's okay)* But look, it's okay ... see? *(grabs the ear and stretches it out for everyone to see)* Yes, I'm sure it was cut off! We came to arrest him, that man called Jesus who has come here from Nazareth, when one of his followers drew a sword from his belt and swung it at me. I didn't see it coming until I felt a horrible pain on the side of my head. Then, like I said, that man Jesus healed my ear! You still don't believe me? Well, just listen to what happened, and then you decide if I'm crazy!

(begins calming down) My name is Malchus, and I am a servant of the high priest, Caiaphas. That's right, I'm an important person, not some country bumpkin or Galilean fisherman, like the guy who cut my ear! *(hand goes up to massage it)* A couple hours ago, my master called me to him and ordered me to gather a detachment of the temple guards. He said the time had come to put an end to the troublemaker named Jesus, a fake healer, blasphemer, and rebel. I had heard of this Jesus — mostly good things about him — but I didn't question my master's orders. He's much more

wise in such matters than I am! I asked where we would find Jesus, and Caiaphas told me with a smile that we would have a guide, a disciple of Jesus named Judas Iscariot. My master told me that Judas would guide us to the right place to make the arrest.

Within a short time we had gathered, issued swords, spears, lanterns, and torches, and met Judas. I didn't like him right from the start, and I could tell some of the soldiers didn't, either. Maybe it was the way he acted, so self-important, or that he boasted about all the silver he had received for payment — more than our pay, and we had to do the dirty work, I might add! Maybe it's just that nobody likes a traitor, even when he's betraying your enemy.

We marched out right away, Judas in the lead, me second, a few other priestly officials close beside me, and the captain of the guard right behind us, followed closely by the troop of soldiers. Our "tour guide" led us out of the city down the road that crosses the Kidron Valley. Then, we ascended up onto the side of the Mount of Olives, taking one of the paths that leads into the Garden of Gethsemane, you know, near the old olive press that is still there. As we approached the garden, Judas told us to be quiet until we came to the place where Jesus often prayed.

Back in the city, I had asked Judas where we were going. When he said Jesus would be in the Garden of Gethsemane, I was surprised. Why out in the olive groves and not hidden inside a house? When we got to the garden, I realized that it made a very good nighttime hiding place. The paths crisscrossed through the grove, there were small clearings and rocky outcrops scattered here and there, and people could get easily confused or even lost if they didn't know their way. Without a guide, it would have been very hard to locate Jesus. Even with one, if Jesus had posted lookouts, they could have seen our torches coming for a long distance and escaped. But for some reason, there were no guards.

The light from our lanterns and torches fell upon a group of men sitting and lying on the ground, groggy as if they had just awakened. In their midst stood one man flanked by three others. When he saw us, he called to the others, "Get up, let us be going. See, my betrayer is at hand." Then he moved toward us and asked, "Who is it you want?" We answered, "Jesus of Nazareth," and then

Judas stepped up to him and kissed his cheek, saying, "Greetings, rabbi!" That was the signal Judas had arranged with us, so we would know for sure which one was Jesus. The one he kissed said, "I am he." As soon as he said that, my knees went weak and I fell to the ground! I wasn't the only one! All of us fell back the same way! I never saw anything like it before! Immediately, we crawled back to our feet.

Again he asked us, "Who is it you want?" Again we said, "Jesus of Nazareth." Again Jesus answered, "I told you that I am he." Then he said, "If you are looking for me, then let these men go," and gestured to his disciples around him. With one hand on my sword, I reached forward with the other soldiers to seize Jesus.

That was when it happened. Blinding pain on the side of my head as my ear was severed. *(holds right hand over right ear again)* I turned my head and saw a disciple named Simon Peter holding a bloody sword in his hand, his fierce eyes shining in the glow of the torches. I was afraid he was going to strike again before I could draw my own sword *(reaches with his left hand toward his right side as if fumbling awkwardly for his sword)*, when I heard Jesus' commanding voice say, "Peter, put your sword back into its place; for all who take the sword will perish by the sword. Do you think that I cannot appeal to my Father, and he will at once send me more than twelve legions of angels? But how then would the scriptures be fulfilled, which say it must happen in this way? Shall I not drink the cup the Father has given me? Enough of this!"

When Jesus reached his hand toward my head, I flinched at first, thinking he was going to harm me further, but his action was done so calmly and confidently, I relaxed. In his hand was my severed ear, though I hadn't even seen him pick it up from the ground. He placed the ear right where it belonged, where it used to be, and lifted his eyes in prayer. I wondered what he was doing, when suddenly I felt a rush of warmth flow like hot oil over the side of my head, through my whole body, and even to the tip of my ear. But wait, how could I feel warmth in my missing ear? Yet, it was true! And not only warmth, but also I could now feel Jesus' hand pressed against my ear. Then I realized one more incredible thing: The pain was gone. Not just less pain, but gone! Not even any tenderness remained! Jesus removed his hand and I reached up with my own hand to feel my ear *(holds his ear again)*, healed and in place, as if nothing had ever happened to it!

Then Jesus chastised us for coming at him with all our weapons. I didn't understand everything he said, but it was obvious he was not going to resist arrest. Peter looked hard at me again — as if to cut off my other ear — then at his master, and then he turned and ran off into the night, with all the other disciples close on his heels.

Some soldiers stepped closer with their ropes to bind Jesus, and the contingent led him back down the Mount of Olives to my master, Caiaphas. Soon Jesus will be tried and condemned, for that is what Caiaphas boasted to me would happen once we caught him.

Yet, I did not accompany them back to my master's house. I have remained behind, here in the garden, because I don't know quite what to do next. Tonight has confused me beyond all measure. I came up here, a servant of the high priest, obeying his orders and convinced that what I was doing was right, a necessary step to protect the nation from the dangerous person Caiaphas accused Jesus of being: a blasphemer, yet Jesus prayed and said he must obey God; a rebel. Yet Jesus refused to fight or allow his disciples to fight; and a fake healer — fake? My eye! I mean, "My ear!" He truly can heal! And why would he heal me, a man who came to arrest him? From what he said, he knows tonight will not go well for him, and yet he had no hatred in him, just compassion, even for his betrayer, Judas, and for me, his arrester, Malchus.

Who is this man? A man of compassion, a man of authority to command his men and be obeyed even in the heat of battle; a man who seeks to do God's will at the cost of his own arrest and likely death; and a man of healing power beyond what is possible! A man hated and feared by many, including my own master. A man I have helped arrest and lead to his certain death.

What should I do about this man? Revile him and help destroy him? Or, perhaps, talk to him and learn more about him and why he acted the way he did tonight? Should I thank him for healing me? Or, should I plead his case before my master? No, Caiaphas wouldn't listen; it would just get me in trouble with him. I can't afford that; Jesus will be gone a day from now, but I will still be working for my master, unless I anger him so much he throws me out on the street. Worse, if I plead for Jesus' life, Caiaphas might accuse me of being one of his followers.

(resignedly, with a sigh) No, it's better I catch up with the others and return to my master. Who is this man, Jesus? Caiaphas says that once Jesus is dead, everyone will soon forget about him, but I know that's not true; for I will never forget him or what he did for me. *(holds ear one last time as he walks away)*

The Centurion At The Cross

(Dressed in Roman uniform, wearing or carrying his helmet, he walks in, removing his helmet if he is wearing it.)

Greetings, my good friends! Thanks for waiting for me! So, how do I look? Good enough to stand before the prefect and answer his questions? *(primps a bit, making sure his armor and clothing are straight)*

(snaps to attention and speaks in a stilted manner, as if addressing the prefect) Gaius Loginus, Centurion of the First Cohort, Sixth Legion, reporting as ordered, Your Excellency. *(salutes stiffly with arm across chest, then chuckles and relaxes slightly)* Yes, I think I'm ready. As a centurion of the Jerusalem cohort, I've seen and talked with Pilate plenty of times, but this is the first time he's actually commanded me to come and face his questioning. After all that's happened today, I'd rather just head back to the barracks and sleep for a couple days.

(looks back over his shoulder) He sure seems disturbed about today's crucifixion, and you know as well as I that executing a few Jews never bothered him before! Like the time that protest broke out because Pilate used the temple's money to pay for an aqueduct; you remember that! He sent a whole troop of us soldiers dressed as Jews into the crowd, and at his signal, we drew our knives and attacked the demonstrators. A lot of Jews were killed that day, and Pilate was pleased with his treachery, not like today, when the deaths of three *(pauses thoughtfully)*, no, make that the death of *one*, has him all agitated.

It's all about the one they call Jesus of Nazareth. There are rumors that Pilate's wife warned him not to execute Jesus; that she told him to have nothing to do with that man, though as governor of Judea, Pilate could hardly have ignored the charges against Jesus. Now Pilate's been asked to release Jesus' body to Jesus' friends for burial, and he wants me to assure him that Jesus is really dead before releasing him! Yeah, right! What a dumb question! *(looks around as if afraid he might be heard)* I mean *(repeats the statement in whisper)*, "What a dumb question!" Prove that a crucified man is dead? I've executed a lot of men on the cross, and I can tell you, so far I ain't ever seen one of them come back to life!

Yeah, that's exactly what *I* think: If Pontius has any doubt, let him examine Jesus' lifeless body for himself! It would only take a moment or two and all his doubts would vanish. The nail holes in the feet and wrists, the wounds from where we beat him, the scars across his scalp from that thorny crown we jammed onto his head. Most of all, the hole where I thrust my spear right up into Jesus' heart. Jesus is dead, all right; he was dead even before I speared him. That's why we didn't bother breaking his legs like we did to those two worthless scum we crucified with him.

I know you weren't up there on Calvary when this all took place; you were probably at the tavern guzzling your cheap wine and playing your games of pebbles and casting lots for money. As certain as I am Jesus is dead, I'm also certain this was the strangest crucifixion I've ever seen! It was strange right from the beginning. When have you ever heard a crowd of Jews scream and demand that we crucify one of *their* religious teachers? That's what they did today, yelling, "Crucify Jesus!"

When Pilate hesitated, the Jews threatened to report Pilate to Caesar if he didn't crucify Jesus, because Jesus was claiming to be their king, and of course, as they cried out, "We have no king but Caesar." *(sarcastically)* Yeah, right! They'd rebel against Caesar in a *heartbeat* if they thought they could get away with it! But their threats worked, and Pilate changed his mind from freeing Jesus to crucifying him.

Then there was the business of the sign over Jesus' head. You know we always write the charges against the condemned, why they are being executed, for public view. You should have seen those self-righteous priests, especially their chief priest, Caiaphas, squirm when they saw the sign Pilate had ordered: "Jesus of Nazareth," it says, "the King of the Jews," written in Greek, Hebrew, *and* Latin. *(chuckles)* Since everybody in town can read Greek or Hebrew, I think Pilate used Latin just to remind the Jews that Rome is in charge over their precious city and country!

I've made many trips to the place of the skull *(says with disdain)*, "Golgotha," as the natives call it, or as we say in our Latin tongue, "Calvary." We usually beat the condemned prisoners and then make them march up the hill, carrying their own crosses, which is only fair, since we have to carry them back down again.

Jesus started out carrying his cross, but he was so weak from the beating he could hardly walk, so I had to recruit a "volunteer" along the way, a Cyrenian, to carry Jesus' cross most of the way. When we got to the top of the hill, the Cyrenian was free to go, but he stayed and acted most strangely, as if he actually cared about the stranger whose cross he carried.

However, the behavior of the condemned man, Jesus, was the most unusual thing. He didn't act like others I have executed. Without exception, the men we crucify scream and curse us, or they beg for mercy, promising us all the gold of Croessus if we only let them go! But Jesus didn't do that. He seemed to accept his crucifixion as if it were his destiny. Though he suffered the same pain and anguish of every other person I've crucified, this man, Jesus, did not curse or beg. Instead, after we hoisted him up on his cross, he looked up into the heavens and prayed that his Father would forgive us! Forgive *us*? *That's* a new one! At first I laughed, but what he said now haunts me. Why do I need forgiveness? Tell me: What have I done wrong? *(anxiety grows)*

(tries to justify himself) Certainly there was nothing wrong with letting my men take his clothing. They don't get paid much for their service in this backwater province of Judea; the least I can do is let them have this fringe benefit. They cast lots to divide Jesus' clothing amongst themselves, but so what? He won't be needing it, now will he?

What is wrong with executing a condemned prisoner? I'm a soldier, after all, and I was just following my orders, doing what the law commands! In spite of Pilate's concerns, I did my job well. Yet, I'll confess to you, my friends, that I feel uneasy as if I *have* done something very wrong, as if I have executed an innocent man! And it's not just my *feelings*, for there are signs in the heavens and in the earth that something great and terrible has happened here today.

Did you see how dark it became today? While we were up on Calvary, the midday sun vanished, and it became like night, as if to

27

show God's displeasure! For three hours it remained dark, but that was just the beginning of signs!

At the very moment Jesus' head slumped in death, the earth quaked all around us, as if the earth were crying out in agony and grief! The ground shook hard, knocking some of us to the ground; near us, we could see huge rocks split into pieces. One of my men screamed that the earth was going to open up and swallow us, trapping us down in Hades with those we have already crucified! Then, a few minutes later, runners came from the city to get Caiaphas and he hurried away with them. Apparently, the earthquake damaged some huge curtain in their precious temple.

What I saw next has shaken me to my core. You know the cemetery that's right below Calvary, the one you can see by looking over the brow of the hill? When I looked down upon that burial ground, I saw — and I swear this is true — graves that had been opened by the earthquake — and there were people — live people — rising from those graves and heading toward the city gate!

No, I've not been drinking! And no, of course, I won't tell Pilate what I saw! He would bust me to a rank trooper in a second. I'll just tell him the truth, at least part of it, that Jesus is definitely dead.

Speaking of Pilate, they're signaling it's time for me to go in. *(turns to go, then turn back to the audience and pauses)* But for myself, I will wonder for the rest of my life: How can this all be happening? What awesome thing has happened here today? Who is this man, this *Jesus*, whom we crucified? No ordinary man's death ever caused the signs we have seen today! We must have done something horribly wrong, for in killing Jesus of Nazareth, I believe we have awakened the anger of God! But if that's so, then we're doomed, for who can stand against God's wrath?

As we nailed Jesus to his cross, he called upon his God to forgive us. Pray for me and for all of us that God heard that prayer! Pray that I will truly be forgiven for what I have done. For today, I have crucified more than a man. Today I have crucified the Son of God! *(walks off stage)*

A Guard At The Tomb

(He enters and stands with his back to the audience. He is wearing some body armor over a tunic with a sword at his side. A hooded robe is pulled up, hiding the head and face from the audience. He turns and looks furtively back and forth a couple times, then pulls the hood down to reveal his face and talks to some people he has agreed to meet with secretly.)

Okay, let's get this over with! I'm only going to say this once, so listen carefully. You wanted to know exactly what happened Sunday morning at the tomb; well, I was there, and I saw it all. I'll tell you what I saw, because it's been troubling me, weighing on my conscience like a heavy stone I've been unable to move. But if you quote me about this, I'll deny it, okay? This meeting *never* happened and I □*never* said what I'm about to tell you, do you understand? Those are my ground rules, because if the chief priests find out I told you, well, the fires of Gehenna will be mild compared to their wrath!

All right, then. You probably know that the tomb where Jesus of Nazareth was laid is empty. That's true. And you've heard the stories going around that his disciples came and stole his body, right? Well, that's not what happened at all. *(looks around again to make sure no one is coming)* Here's what really happened.

It was the sabbath, and as usual, I was on duty at the temple, just one of the many guards in my detachment charged with keeping order there and keeping Gentiles out. There was the usual stream of devout worshipers, and the sacrifices offered by the priests were sending their acrid smoke up into heaven. This day was different than most; there was a lot of buzz about the earthquakes that had happened the day before, and the rumor was that the curtain in the holy of holies had been torn, though none of us was allowed in there to actually see for ourselves.

Then, about midday, one of the chief priests summoned a small troop of us to report for a special assignment. I was curious — what could it be? Perhaps to guard a caravan of spices or money on the way to the temple from another land? Or perhaps a Gentile had been seen sneaking into the temple, an offense punishable by death and enforced by the Romans, as well as by us Jews. Or, I thought, maybe we were to be bodyguards for Caiaphas on a journey somewhere.

We arrived at the priests' quarters, eager for a break from the boredom that is a soldier's greatest enemy. Imagine our surprise and disappointment when he gave us our orders: We were to guard a dead body! Oh, the orders sounded more noble than that *(repeating as it was said, a little stilted)*: "You will escort an official of the temple out of the city to the tombs near Golgotha, where you will take position at the entrance to the tomb of Joseph of Arimathea. The official shall seal the tomb entrance with the official seal and then you will guard the entrance for three days to prevent anyone from carrying away the corpse." Like I said, we were to guard a dead body! He explained that he and some other priests had met with Pontius Pilate that morning for permission to post a guard at the tomb. Buried inside was a man named Jesus of Nazareth, condemned and crucified as a blasphemer, and the priests wanted to make absolutely sure his body stayed buried. Apparently, Jesus had predicted he would come back to life in three days, and the priests wanted to make sure his disciples didn't steal his body and then claim he arose.

We saluted, gathered our equipment and supplies, and within half an hour we had formed up to escort the priestly official to the tomb. The march was uneventful, though I couldn't help but notice on the way that some tombs we passed were broken open. According to the official, that had happened during the earthquake the day before. I got shivers when I looked in one of the tombs we passed and saw that it was empty. Had someone stolen that body, too?

We finally reached the garden and gathered at the tomb we were to guard. At the priest's orders, we rolled back the heavy stone covering its entrance to make sure the body was in place. It was. I noticed it had not been anointed with the perfumes and spices that are usually lavished on the dead; instead, the body just lay there in its white grave cloths, body and face both covered. My thought at the moment was, "This guy's not going anywhere!"

We rolled the stone back into place, and the official stepped forward with his wax, fire, and the official seal of the high priest. He melted the wax over the stone where it met the rock wall, and pressed the seal into the soft wax until it hardened. Then he turned away and headed back to the temple under escort of two of the guards. Those two would be back for a later shift.

So, there we were, standing around, guarding a tomb. We looked at each other, and after a few smiles, we started laughing and made ourselves comfortable. We cast lots to decide who would take each shift, then began to joke about our assignment. At first we joked about which was our real job, to keep the disciples out, or to keep Jesus in. We joked about how many of us it would take to hold the stone closed if he did come alive and try to get out. Someone suggested another earthquake could break the tomb open. We laughed, but for a few seconds I felt a chill again, when I remembered the empty grave we passed earlier.

We asked ourselves, "Why would anyone steal a dead body to prove someone was alive again?" We laughed as we imagined his disciples trying to pass off a dead body as being alive. Showing a dead body wouldn't convince *anyone* Jesus was alive, nor would his absence from a tomb. Eventually, people would know it was a hoax.

We talked some more. One of the guards asked if we had seen Caiaphas' servant, Malchus, this weekend. Another said he did see Malchus, and that the servant couldn't stop showing everybody his ear and talking about it being cut off and Jesus healing it. The guard said, "Malchus almost talked *my* ear off, he was so wound up about it!" We laughed and told some ear jokes.

Our discussion then ranged from Malchus to the other strange events of that Friday, to the even stranger assignment we now had — to guard a dead body. We all agreed, something unusual, even supernatural, was going on. These were signs that surely meant something; we just didn't know what.

The day dragged on. We joked and told stories for a while, then we got tired and bored of this duty. Obviously, nothing was going to happen. The disciples were a bunch of cowards: The word was that they had run and hidden when Jesus was arrested. And when the head disciple had been spotted at Caiaphas' house and people had confronted him? Well, he denied even knowing Jesus. No, we wouldn't have any trouble; if someone got up enough courage to come to the tomb, the sight of us guarding it would certainly scare them away. We believed it was going to be an uneventful couple days. Were we wrong!

Oh, Saturday was fine — a long day spent without incident. We guarded the tomb but saw nothing extraordinary. No one came to the tomb and no one left it. There were just us guards, some standing, some sitting, some winning a denarius or two by casting lots, and some losing that same denarius or two. Others caught naps to get ready for the night shift. We did the usual things soldiers do in such a situation to pass the time.

Sunday morning was when it happened. I had just been awakened by one of the other guards and told it was my time to get up and take his place at the tomb's entrance. He was beat and ready to catch a couple hours of sleep. I crawled out from under the warmth of my cloak and stood up in the cold, predawn air. After exchanging a grunt with the other on-duty guards, I took my place just to one side of the large stone that covered the tomb's entrance.

When the earthquake hit, I was taken completely by surprise. The ground shook violently under my feet and I fell to my knees. As the tremors continued, I could barely keep my balance enough to stay on all fours, even as I watched the other guards fall against the rock wall and onto the ground. Those who had been asleep awoke with a start and shouted cries of alarm, not knowing what was happening. Not that I was doing any better! My helmet was off my head, my spear lay somewhere out of reach, and I was regretting having eaten that spiced lamb for supper.

No sooner had the tremors subsided, than the unbelievable happened. Suddenly, a bright light appeared, lighting up everything around us so brightly we had to shield our eyes from its glory. It was as if we were staring into the sun, but it was barely dawn! Then, in the midst of the light, we saw *him*, a shining being like a man, only larger and more powerful, an angel sent from God, coming straight toward me! There was no resisting his power. I crawled out of his way as he moved to the tomb. With powerful arms he reached out, took ahold of the stone, and rolled it back like it was nothing more than a loaf of bread. Then the angel rose up in the air and took a seat upon the stone. He sat there glaring at us, as if challenging us to stop him.

But none of us could do or say a thing. I began to shake with fear unlike anything I had ever felt before. It was the power of God that filled the clearing in which we knelt and crawled at that moment, a power that I can barely describe to you now, except to say that it overwhelmed us, and we fell flat on the ground like dead men. I know, you don't believe me! But I swear to you it's true! I was not dreaming; I was fully awake. I hadn't been drinking, either; I was totally sober! And I'm not crazy *(pauses)*, though I will never be the same after all this.

When we came to, the angel was still seated there, but as I half-walked, half-crawled away from the tomb, I could see the stone bench inside where Jesus' body had lain. It was empty! His body was gone! I grabbed my spear and helmet and joined the others as we hurried away from the tomb and the garden and almost ran the distance back to the temple to report what had happened.

Needless to say, the chief priests were *not* pleased. We expected the harshest discipline they could heap upon us, but to our surprise, they gave each of us some money, a lot of money, and told us what to do: "You're to say, 'His disciples came during the night and stole him away while we were asleep.' And don't worry, we'll make sure you don't get in trouble for it!"

So that is the story we have told. I'm sure people believe us. Our stories are all consistent, and what else would they believe? That an angel came and rolled the stone away? That Jesus' body got up on its own and walked out of that tomb? That Jesus, who had been crucified, dead, and buried for three days somehow fulfilled his promise to rise again from the dead? No, people will *want* to believe us.

However, my thoughts have troubled me ever since the events of that early Sunday morning, and now my conscience aches for spreading lies about what happened. I'm telling you now because the truth needs to be known ... because *I* need to know the truth, too. Who is this man? Who is this Jesus that God would darken the skies and shake the earth at his death? Who is Jesus, that God would send an angel to open his tomb? Who is Jesus, that he should prophesy his own resurrection and then fulfill it? I want to know the truth — I need to know the truth! For I have encountered the power and glory of God, and now I must know more about the man I could not keep in his grave. *(turns and exits silently)*

Series 2

Women Of The Promise

Eve

(Eve walks in holding a small, old-looking shovel or hand trowel. She wears rough clothing with a fur or faux fur wrap as part of her costume. Her face is dirty. Her attitude is somber, as if she has been crying.)
It wasn't supposed to be like this! This wasn't supposed to happen! My Adam is ... he's dead! I have never known this world, or life itself, without him! But now, he's gone! I've just buried him, back there *(points behind her with sweep of her arm)* on a hill overlooking the river where we used to sit together and watch the water flow past. I dug the hole with tools that were meant only to till and cultivate the ground — to grow food and sustain life — tools now pressed into more somber work at life's end. I can't tell you how hard it was to shovel the dirt over his lifeless body. My beloved Adam ... gone ... good-bye, my love, I will miss you so much.

Did you know we were together for over 930 years? I remember each and every anniversary well — all 930 of them! How hard it was to give something new for each one! After paper, silver, gold, and diamonds, we ran out of ideas, though I told Adam that jewelry was always appropriate!

I never thought this day would really come, even after the Lord God declared we would die because we disobeyed him. He had warned us about it, but we hardly understood what death meant — around us there was only harmony and life. When we sinned, God told us that we were only dust, and to dust we would return. Now that is being fulfilled, as Adam returns to the dust from which he was formed.

Oh, but life wasn't always so somber! I remember many good times, beginning that first day that I woke up, the first day of my life — not as a baby, like all of you did, but fully grown and conscious. I woke up and sat up, then stood up, amazed at all the sights and sounds and smells around me. I looked at myself, and moved my fingers and hands and my toes and feet, my arms and legs. I looked to one side and then to the other, marveling at just being alive in a brand new world full of things to experience.

That's when I saw *him* — the *man* — lying on the ground and stirring as he woke up from a deep sleep. Who was this strange creature, who looked something like me, yet different? At first, I didn't know who or even *what* he was. You might say, I didn't know him from Adam!

The Lord himself made the introductions and told us that we were now husband and wife. From Adam's wide-eyed look, and the smile plastered across his face, I could tell he approved of the idea, and so did I, though I wasn't quite sure why.

I just trusted the Lord and what he said to the man and me. The Lord told me that I had been formed from one of Adam's ribs while he slept. I used to tease Adam about that missing rib; I would touch the spot where the rib had been and warn him to be careful not to fall asleep again — who knows what might be missing next time? Or I would tell him I was obviously more perfect than he because I had all *my* ribs — besides, since I was made after Adam, God *must* have saved the best for last!

The Lord commanded us to multiply, but he wasn't talking about doing math. I asked Adam if he had any more ribs to spare to make some new people, but his answer was that he had a better idea. And did he ever!

Those earliest days were wonderful, as we talked and got to know each other so well. Our relationship with each other and with God was perfect — no lies, no anger, no secrets or selfishness — just love and enjoyment. We were like two big children, innocently exploring a new world, as we walked and ran through the beautiful garden where God had placed us. The green of the lush vegetation cooled us and filled our eyes, and the bounty of delicious fruits and vegetables filled our stomachs. It was paradise on earth, a paradise that would never end. Or so we thought.

Then came the serpent, and the innocent paradise came crashing down. Oh, I know, it wasn't just the serpent's fault, though when God confronted us I did try to blame it all on the snake. I admit now it was our fault, Adam's and mine. For a long time I blamed myself, mostly, because I was the first to eat the forbidden fruit, and at first Adam blamed me, too. He complained to God, saying, "The woman whom you gave to be with me, she gave me fruit from the tree and I ate." How that hurt! For my husband to accuse me before God, speaking as if he wished God had never brought me to him; for the first time our oneness was broken, a casualty of our first sin. Later, Adam accepted his own guilt in the matter after we were forced to leave the garden, to work and struggle together among the thorns and weeds of the earth for barely enough to eat.

I wish I could go back and live that horrible day of disobedience all over again and this time refuse the temptation. If only I hadn't listened to the serpent's lies. If only I had trusted God, instead of doubting him. If only I had been content with the paradise the Lord had given us and not coveted the one thing he withheld. If only my pride hadn't wanted me to become like God himself ... if only, if only ... but it's too late. I can't go back now and do it right.

Yet, in the midst of God's judgment, even as he pronounced his curses upon us and all his creation, there was something that God said that caught my attention, just a short sentence that stood out from the rest of his words like a cool oasis in the hot desert. When God cursed the serpent, he said these words I'll never forget: "I will put enmity between you and the woman, and between your offspring and hers; he will strike your head, and you will strike his heel."

In those words I heard the promise of a child, a man to be born of a woman, a man who would destroy the devilish serpent, and by doing so bring salvation to us all. How I hoped that child would be born right away, to spare us the consequences of our sin, even to save us from having to die. So I longed for the son of the promise.

Later, when I had my first child, Adam called me Eve, which means, "mother of all living," because all people to be born on earth would come from me or from those born to me. It was a new thing for me to be pregnant, and to know I was carrying a new human being inside me. There had been only us two, and now another was coming!

Was this the one promised by God? The offspring of a woman, of me, who would crush the serpent and save us from the horrible sin we had committed?

I was sure it had to be, and so I named him Cain, which means "brought forth," because I believed I had brought forth the Savior, the promised one. How wrong I was! At first there was the joy of having a baby, and watching him grow and develop into a strong young man, and the further joy of watching his brother, Abel, and his sisters and other brothers be born. But soon, that joy turned to ashes in my mouth, when Cain murdered Abel, his own brother.

God gave us these animal skins *(takes hold of the fur)* to cover us after we sinned, saying our clothing of leaves was not enough, that sin required death and the shedding of blood. Now I know dearly how true that is. Adam and Abel have paid with their lives, as eventually all of us will. Soon, it will be my time, too.

So I wait for the day of my promised Savior to come. Will it be soon? Or is it already too late, now that Adam is gone? Will I ever get to see Adam again? Is there hope even in the midst of death? Will God forgive us for what we did?

I once failed because I doubted God's word of warning; let me never doubt his word of promise! Let the promised Savior come, and whether I am still here when he comes, or if I go to be with my husband first, still I will trust in God. For I am Eve, a woman of the promise. *(turns and exits)*

Sarah

(Sarah enters purposefully, carrying a bowl, plate, or cup and is headed somewhere in a hurry. She calls out as if answering someone in the direction she's headed.)

Just a minute! Be patient! I'm coming, Abram! *(stops and shakes her head as if disgusted with herself for getting his name wrong)* I mean, Abraham!

(turns to the audience and talks to them) I can never get his new name right! All my life, since I was a little girl, I knew him as Abram — for 99 years he was Abram, and now suddenly, he had to go and change his name to Abraham. He said God gave him the new name, which means "father of many," because God promised to make him the father of many nations. Nations, mind you! Quite a thing to promise a childless old man who was married to a childless old woman! At least, we *were* childless, until ... until that changed, too.

Our whole life together has been one of many changes, big changes, ever since that day back in Mesopotamia when Abe — Abraham — was visited by the Lord and told to get up and go to a new land that God would show him. Until then, things had been stable and predictable. We lived in Haran and did pretty well for ourselves, except for not having any children. Our nephew, Lot, lived with us, as did many servants and workers, and we could have expected a comfortable retirement there, but when Abe turned 75, he came to me and said we needed to pack up our tents and belongings because we were moving to Canaan.

At first I thought his turning 75 must have triggered a mid-life crisis, you know, time to buy a new camel, dye his hair and beard dark again, lose some weight ... but he spoke with such passion and conviction, I knew something amazing must have happened! He said the Lord God had come to him and called him to go to a new land; that he would make a great nation of him and that through him all nations of the world would be blessed. The world! I was dumbfounded, but did as he told me and soon we were on the way to the land of the Canaanites.

More changes! First we stayed at Shechem, in northern Canaan, then moved down to Egypt where there was food and water for us and our flocks. Then, back to the Negev, and finally to a place Abraham called Bethel, which means "house of God." After that, there came more changes, as our nephew, Lot, left us to move to a place named Sodom, near Gomorrah, because he said he wanted to live in a city that had a future!

Then Abraham changed *my name*! I used to be Sarai, which was good enough for me for almost ninety years, but now he called me Sarah. My name now means "princess" *(postures and preens a little)*, which actually isn't bad! It had something to do with God's promise that I would become the *mother* of many nations.

There was a problem: All this talk of Abraham and me becoming parents of many nations was fine, but that's the one area where our lives hadn't changed. We still did not have any children. Ten years had gone by since God had promised Abraham that he would have children, but there was no sign of that happening. Was God wrong? Had Abraham misunderstood the promise? Had we been faithful enough, or had God changed his mind? Should we appeal to the many other gods of the people of Canaan? Could they help us instead?

No, we would trust the true God over all other gods, even though his promise was so outlandish, so impossible it would take an all-powerful God to accomplish it. For God promised not just a son, and not just many descendants from many nations, he also promised one special descendent he called "the Seed." One seed, one offspring, through whom all the nations of the world would be blessed. That had to mean a Savior, a Messiah, like the one promised long ago to Eve. Was it possible that this Savior would come from us and our descendants?

We would trust God and take him at his word, but maybe, we thought, he needed a little help. If I couldn't bear any children, maybe someone else could for me, a surrogate mother, so to speak, to bear Abraham's promised son. After all, that was the custom of many of the tribes around us, that an infertile wife could provide someone else to become the mother of her children, so I decided to send my handmaiden, Hagar, to Abraham.

What a mistake that was! Sure, she became pregnant, which itself was something of a miracle since Abraham was 86 years old by now, but once she gave birth to her son, Ishmael, we had all kinds of problems.

First, Hagar went around flaunting her son, Ishmael, and reminding everyone just whose son he *really* was, which made me so jealous! Then, she started treating me with contempt, *me*, her mistress! I became so angry! I know it was wrong, but no longer did I want Ishmael to become Abraham's heir — I just wanted her and the boy to go away. I stormed up to Abraham and demanded he get rid of them and so he did, sending them away into the desert with just a bag of water. Later she came back and submitted to me, saying the Lord's angel had appeared to her and commanded it.

Neither Ishmael nor his seed would be the promised one. God had someone else in mind. But who?

Abraham went and prayed and asked the Lord if one of our male servants was to be the inheritor of the promise. God said that was not to be, a son born to Abraham and to *me* would be the one. The Lord took him out under the night sky and showed him the sweep of stars shining above him. "Your descendants will number many more than these stars," he said, "more than the sands on the seashore."

Then came the day, when my husband was 99 years old and I was 89, when we had three special visitors. Being ever the gracious host, Abraham welcomed them in and ordered me to bring them some food. While I was preparing it, I overheard one guest tell Abe that one year from then I would give birth to his promised son. I couldn't help but laugh when I heard that! I would be ninety years old! How could I know the joy of giving birth to a child, of nursing him, and watching him grow?

Well, you can guess what happened. One year later I gave birth to a baby boy, and we named him Isaac, which appropriately means "laughter." I guess the last laugh was on me! We learned for certain that with God nothing is impossible!

(becomes somber) That is a lesson I need to remember, for the Lord has given Abraham — and me — one final test. That's why

I'm taking this food to Abraham right now; he and Isaac are leaving on a journey together. The Lord has commanded him to take our son, our only son, Isaac, the son whom we love, up onto a mountain that is a three-day journey from here. When they get there *(finds it hard to continue)* ... when they get there ... Abraham is to offer our son as a sacrifice, a burnt offering to God. *(pauses)* Abraham hasn't told Isaac what he has to do. At first, he wasn't even going to tell me, but Abraham never could keep any secrets from me.

We spent last night in prayer and in tears, wondering how God, who has always blessed us so richly, could possibly command us to give up our only begotten son to him. Isn't Isaac the son of promise? Isn't he the one to begin the fulfillment of many nations of descendants? Isn't the Messiah to come through his line?

Abram ... Abraham ... and I don't understand. We love our son so much, and God knows how long we've waited for him to bless our home with the sound of laughter — the sound of Isaac — only now, he wants to take him away. How can it be? Why, except to test our faith, to see if we really trust God's promise no matter what would stand in the way? Could not the one who gave a son to an elderly couple like us, also return our son from the dead? Could he not provide a Savior for Isaac?

I am glad I am not Abraham today and face what he must do. I also know, that with God, nothing is impossible, and so I will trust in him. For my name is Sarah, and I am a woman of the promise.

Rebecca

(She sits at a table on which sits a pot. She is stirring the "stew" inside and after a moment she ladles some out and sips it with a loud, slurping sound.)
Aaaah! Just about right ... maybe a little more coriander seed. Goat stew needs a pinch of coriander seed, don't you agree? *(drops in a pinch, stirs, and sips again)* There, that should do it. Now it tastes perfect! It's my husband, Isaac's, absolute favorite dish, which is what I'm counting on! You see, my son, Jacob, and I have a little trick to play on Isaac — a surprise, sort of, and it all depends on this stew tasting just right. It depends on this stew and on a certain strip of goatskin.

You look confused. Well, don't worry. I know what I'm doing — sort of. At least I know *why* I'm doing it; it all has to do with Isaac and the blessing he is supposed to give to one of our sons, Jacob or Esau. That blessing is all-important because it determines just who will become the next leader of our family and inherit our wealth and ... and even receive the promise of God. That's why this stew has to be just right, so Jacob gets the blessing! Oh, you still don't understand? Okay *(looks around furtively to make sure Isaac isn't listening)*, I'll tell you, but you must promise not to breathe a word of this to Isaac. *(points her spoon threateningly at the audience)*

The problem is, I have two sons. Now that doesn't seem like a problem, and I never thought it would be, when I was barren and didn't have any children. Back then, if you had told me I was going to have two strong sons, and twins at that, I would have danced and sung a song of joy! I *am* glad I had them, but from the very beginning, there have been, well, problems. While I was still pregnant with them, they fought together in my womb! I know it's hard to believe, but it's true. You've heard of babies kicking; these two boys threw punches and wrestled, too! I recalled the words of the Lord who had predicted their birth, saying, "Two nations are in your womb; and two peoples will be separated from your body; one people shall be stronger than the other; and the older shall serve the younger."

Finally, the day of their birth came, and even then, their struggle continued. Esau was born first, but even as he came out, there was his brother, Jacob, close behind, grasping firmly onto Esau's heel. Did I mention they were twins? Well, not identical twins like you sometimes see, not at all. Esau, the firstborn, was all covered in red hair, almost like animal fur or a hairy coat. Jacob looked more normal.

As they grew, the rivalry continued, but they followed different paths. Esau became a great hunter, spending time out in the field and bringing back wild game to eat, which made Isaac very happy. Soon, Esau was Isaac's favorite ... but not mine! I've always preferred Jacob. I know a mother *should* love all her children equally, but God had said that the older child, Esau, would serve the younger one, Jacob, so if God can favor one, then I guess I can, too.

It's not just that I enjoy talking with Jacob more, it's that Jacob seems much more interested in the future. More interest in the stories Isaac and *his* father, Abraham, told around the fire, about God's promise that many nations and descendants more numerous than the stars would come from our family. Or about the trip Isaac and Abraham took into the mountains where Abraham prepared to sacrifice Isaac to God! Only God's direct intervention, by sending an angel to stop the sacrifice, saved him and allowed him to be my future husband. Jacob always loved those stories; but as for Esau, he'd always rather go hunting.

In fact, it was one of Esau's hunting trips that most opened my eyes to the difference between them. Esau had been out on an extended hunt and returned home famished. It seems he hadn't gotten any game. As soon as he arrived back in camp, he smelled something wonderful cooking — a tasty lentil soup made by Jacob, using one of my recipes, of course! Jacob offered Esau the soup in exchange for Esau's birthright as the firstborn, a birthright that promised Esau twice the inheritance of Jacob, now freely given in exchange for a mess of pottage. How cheaply did Esau dispose of his birthright! He deserved to give it to someone who took it seriously, and that better man was Jacob.

I was overjoyed at Jacob's fortune, but there is one more thing he needs to be secure as the true successor and inheritor of Isaac, and that is *the blessing*. When Isaac gives his blessing to a son, God's blessing also will go with it. Isaac will be speaking for God, and the blessing he promises will come true. Jacob needs the blessing of the firstborn to go with the purchased birthright, but here's the rub: Isaac will give that blessing to only one son, and that son is Esau.

If Esau were righteous, I wouldn't feel so strongly about helping Jacob get Isaac's blessing, but Esau has despised the family as well as his birthright. When he turned forty, he married two Hittite women. He said they were both twenty, so they added up just right! He and those women have caused nothing but turmoil in our family for Isaac and me, and yet Isaac didn't want to scold his favorite son for what he did. Worse, now that Isaac is over 100 years old and knows his death is near, he feels an urgency before he dies to bless Esau.

But now, listen! *(excitedly)* Just a short while ago I was approaching my husband when I heard him say to Esau, "Take your quiver and your bow, and go out to the field and hunt game for me; prepare a savory dish for me such as I love, and bring it to me that I may eat, so that my soul may bless you before I die." When Esau grabbed his gear and headed out into the fields to do as Isaac instructed, I knew we had to act fast before Esau returned!

I rushed back to Jacob and urged him to bring me a goat from the flock, and now, while Esau is out hunting, I made this dish just the way Isaac likes it. He won't know the difference! *(stirs the pot again, more quickly)* Then, Jacob will pretend he is Esau when he takes him the stew, and since poor, old Isaac is blind, he will bless Jacob, thinking it's Esau.

The only danger is if Isaac touches Jacob's arms and feels his smooth skin instead of Esau's hairy fur ... so I told Jacob to get pieces of goatskin with the fur still on them and put them over his hands and neck. That way, if Isaac touches him, he'll feel the hair and think it's Esau. I hope it works!

I know, you don't have to tell me. It's deceitful to fool my husband in something so important to him. But you have to understand, it's even more important that Isaac not bless Esau, and that Jacob gets the blessing instead. God foretold it when he said the older son would serve the younger, so we're only doing God's will. Besides, Esau has shown himself to be unworthy of the promise given by God to Abraham and Isaac. He despised the birthright and shamed the family with his marriages.

Now it will be up to Jacob, the heel-grabber, to grab the blessing, just as he grabbed the birthright. The promise of God and his purposes must not be allowed to fail. We must do our part if all the nations of the world are to be blessed.

(emphatically) Therefore, I will not be deterred. I *will* help Jacob get the blessing the Lord God wants him to have, because I am Rebecca, and I am a woman of the promise!

Rahab

(Rahab runs in carrying a long, red cord or rope. She acts urgently, but with purpose. She shouts to the audience.)

All right! Be quiet now, and do just what I say, and we'll all be safe! Don't be afraid; I know what to do! *(ties one end of the rope to the front of the altar rail or other visible place)* There! They ordered me to hang a red cord from my window when they come, so they would know which house is mine. They promised to spare my life, and you, my family, if I hung out this cord. I hope they keep their word, because they're on the way, right now! Thousands, no, hundreds of thousands of them! *(looks out the window and gestures in the direction of what she sees)* The Israelite army is marching straight here! They'll be close enough to attack any minute now! I sure hope they can see this cord up here on top of the massive city walls.

(looks back inside at the audience) Hush! Don't bother praying to those idols you've got hanging around your necks; they're just stone and wood. If you want help, you better pray to Yahweh, the God of the Israelites, because that's the one you've got to worry about! That's the one who parted the Red Sea, destroyed Pharaoh's army, and annihilated the Amorites. I'm convinced he is the true God, and he's coming right now with his people to level our mighty city of Jericho! Do you think our thick walls and mighty warriors will save us? Don't count on it! Only the true God, Yahweh, can save us, if he wants to!

You're looking at me funny ... What? How do I know so much about the Israelites and their God? Remember when those two men came and stayed here a short while ago? No, that's right, you probably don't. *(humbly)* Considering my business, a lot of men have stayed here; why would you notice two more? These two were the guys the soldiers came looking for. Now you remember, don't you? How our king somehow learned about two Israelite spies in the city and sent his troops here looking for them. They didn't find them because I had hidden the spies up on the roof in piles of flax, and then I lied to the soldiers, saying the men had already escaped from the city.

The soldiers left, and the spies told me about their God and all the miracles he had done for them in the desert across the Jordan. My heart melted like wax when I heard of Yahweh's awesome power. Who could stand against him? Finally, the coast was clear, so I let the spies out and gave them safe directions to escape back to their people, after demanding they spare our lives, too.

Don't look at me like that; I had to protect the spies. It was the right thing to do, and the only way for us to be spared when the Israelites and their God come to destroy this city. *(looks back "outside" the window)* And here they come now!

I know you can't see them from where you are, so I'll describe for you what's happening out there. It looks like locusts covering the ground, but it's the Israelite soldiers, marching in a huge procession. They're not charging the city walls, or aiming their bows and arrows at us, either. *(looks puzzled)* It looks like they're just marching *around* the city. Aren't they going to attack? Now wait a minute — *there's* something different! Following the mass of soldiers is a group of men dressed like priests; I think they are priests! Seven priests, it looks like — and they're carrying seven trumpets made from rams' horns. Now they're putting the trumpets to their mouths, and — can you hear that? They're blowing the horns! Then, following them is something I've never seen before, a golden chest or box, an ark of some kind, being carried by priests who are holding long poles beneath the box. It must be an important object to them! At the end of the procession is a rear guard of more soldiers — and still the priests are blowing their trumpets. But still they're not attacking!

(turns away from the window, disappointed and puzzled) I don't understand; why haven't the Israelites attacked? Are they afraid of us, of Jericho's solid stone walls and trained soldiers? No, it can't be that ... they've already defeated mighty armies on their way here.

Are they afraid of the gods of this land, or that their God might not be so powerful in this country? No, I believe Yahweh is God in heaven above and on earth beneath, and so does Israel. They have witnessed firsthand his miraculous power. Israel would not fear our puny idols.

So, if they fear neither us nor their gods, then why hesitate to attack? It must be because they're waiting for their God to say the time is right. That means they trust in him; that he will give them the victory, in his way, in his time.

What would it be like to know and worship the true God and to listen for his word of command? To trust him so much you could endure any challenge? To pray and know you will actually be heard? And to know that your God has the power to answer your prayer? Not like our so-called gods made of stone and wood! I've seen a woodcarver cut a piece of wood in half. From one half, he carves a beautiful idol. The other half, he throws into the fire to keep warm. What kind of god is that?

No, that's not the kind of god I want to worship. I don't want to worship false gods anymore. I want to worship and know the true God, Yahweh. And, if he does spare me when this city is destroyed, I *will* serve him.

(suddenly looks worried as a thought occurs to her) But will the true God accept me as one of his? After all, I'm not an Israelite! He is the God of Israel; why should he bother with a foreigner like me? Look how he has blessed Israel and increased their numbers like the stars of the night sky. He doesn't really need one more, especially, one like me.

The spies said their God is a holy God, moral and righteous, unlike the pagan deities of this city. He has given his people commandments, carved by his own finger on tablets of stone. These laws forbid stealing, lying, murdering, and doing the very thing that has been my livelihood since I became a young woman. If Yahweh demands holiness and righteous living of his followers, then why would he want me? If he wants to save someone in Jericho, why not save someone more upright and righteous? Is this righteous God also a loving and forgiving God? If he is, could he ever forgive *me* for all my sins, even if I promise I will never go back to that way of life?

Could he forgive me for worshiping false gods? Yahweh has every right to say to me, "Rahab, you have believed in the false gods of wood and stone all your life; let *them* deliver you now!"

When you come right down to it, I don't have much going for me, much worth God saving. I'm an outsider, a sinner, a worshiper of false gods. How can I stand before the true God as one of his? Yet, that is what I must do, because I know now that he is the true God of heaven and earth, and there is no other. Only in him is there a promise of deliverance and salvation. I will trust that promise, for only by his mercy will I be saved.

So, whether he accepts me or not, whether he ever sends the Israelites to take this city *(gestures "outside")* or not, whether the spies see *(picks up end of the cord)* this red cord and remember to spare me, or not, I will trust him. Whether he forgives my sins, or not, still I will put my trust in him and worship him *(resolutely)*, for I am Rahab, and I want to be a woman of the promise!

Mary, Mother Of Jesus

(She begins by standing in front of the cross as if watching Jesus dying. She turns away in grief and walks/staggers over to the stage center. One hand is holding a cloth to her face, and the other reaching out as if finding her way. She has been weeping.)

He's dead! My son, Yeshua, Jesus, is dead! *(stops to weep and then regains enough composure to continue)* How could they have done this to him? What did he do to deserve death? Don't they know about all the people he healed, the blind he gave sight to, the lame who walk, the people he raised from the *dead*? Don't they know about his great love for all of us? How could they all hate him so much — enough to ... to do this? *(gestures back at the cross)*

If only they knew him as I know him, this wouldn't be happening. If only they knew about his love and his goodness, or about his always taking care of other people who needed help, never worrying about himself or using his powers to make himself rich or powerful. The Romans said he claimed to be a king who might oppose Caesar. They mocked him, jammed a crown of thorns down onto his head, and nailed a sign above his head on the cross, a sign announcing him as king of the Jews. If he was an earthly king, he would have fought, but he didn't! Let the Romans tell me: Where is his army? Where are the spears and shields? Where are the chariots and horses? Horses? All he ever rode was a humble donkey!

But it's not just the Romans. Our own religious leaders, the Sanhedrin, hate Jesus, too. They charged that Jesus threatened to destroy the temple, which wasn't true; and that he claimed to be the Son of God; in that at least, they are right! The leaders called it blasphemy for Jesus to say he was God, and it would be, unless Jesus *is* God. Then, their rejection of him would itself be blasphemous! I know, as no one else could know, that Jesus *is* God's own Son, for he had no earthly father. The angel told me my firstborn would be from God himself, and though I soon learned that I was with child, no man had touched me, not even my husband, Joseph, before Jesus was born.

(looks up sharply) What angel? Gabriel, the angel who visited me when I was a young woman, back in Nazareth. Oh, I know, so many people in our modern age don't believe in angels anymore, but they are real, special messengers from the Lord our God. And that day, the message brought to me was one of incredible joy, a message almost unbelievable to a poor girl from Nazareth. After all, as you Judeans always say, "Can anything good come from Nazareth?"

That day, the angel told me, "Do not be afraid, Mary; for you have found favor with God. And now, you will conceive in your womb and bear a son, and you will name him Jesus. He will be great, and will be called the Son of the Most High." I asked the angel, "How can this be, since I am a virgin?" The angel answered and said to me, "The Holy Spirit will come upon you, and the power of the Most High will overshadow you; and for that reason the holy Child shall be called the Son of God."

Me, Mary, the one to give birth to the Son of God? To the Savior? How could it be? I can't tell you how overwhelmed I felt, to be chosen by God to bear the Messiah! Why, that has been the dream of every believing woman for every generation since Eve herself! Now, I was to be the one — I, not Eve, or Sarah, or Rebecca, or even Rahab, nor countless thousands of other women, but *me*. I had no idea why God should choose me, but he had, and slowly the realization swept over me that I would bear a great responsibility to go with the honor bestowed on me. On that day *(joyfully)*, I sang out with joy that all generations would call me blessed! *(turns suddenly somber)* I could not have foreseen the agony and horror of this day. *(looks back at the cross)* On this day no one would want to take my place, or my son's!

Was this how Eve felt when they brought her dead son, Abel, to her, the victim of his brother's hatred? Is this how Sarah felt, when Abraham took off with Isaac to sacrifice him, their only son, as an offering that God had demanded? Isaac returned alive! What joy Sarah must have felt at that moment to see her son again! If only my son could have been spared, too! If only Jesus could come back from the dead! How could I have known it would end like this, when it all began with so much promise?

There was the promise that comes with every child who is born: of a full lifetime ahead. What joy to see him grow from a newborn, cuddled and nursing in my arms, then to see him run with the other children, later to see him study for his bar mitzvah, and finally to become a full-grown man, a carpenter, and a rabbi. How much more of life lay ahead of him!

There was the promise told us at his birth, relayed to us by the shepherds of Bethlehem, and later by the visiting magi, of Jesus' special nature and destiny: Jesus was Messiah, Lord, and King.

There were the promises Jesus himself made, that the kingdom of God was now upon us; that he had brought us forgiveness of sins and eternal life. He promised us God's love and showed it in so many miraculous ways. Jesus' life was so full of promise! Why did it have to end?

(pauses, despondently, head hanging down in her hands, then lifts her head with growing excitement) In all the horror this day has brought, I almost forgot that there was one more promise he made! Yes, he told us many times that he had to come to Jerusalem to die like the prophets of old. I couldn't accept that and tried to pretend it wouldn't happen. Some of the disciples even tried to talk him out of coming here, but he insisted, even when he could have run away and hidden instead. He talked about the cross, saying we must take up our crosses and follow him. He said he had to come and suffer many things and even die.

Even as he told us that, he connected his death to a promise: He said he came to give his life as a ransom for many. John the Baptist called Jesus the Lamb of God who takes away the sins of the world. Somehow, in some way, Jesus died for us.

I remember now, he also promised that this would not be the end! He said that just as Jonah emerged from the belly of the whale after three days, so he would come back in three days! Other times he said it plainly, that he would be rejected by the elders and the chief priests and the scribes, and be killed, and after three days rise again. But how? He raised others from the dead, but who will raise him?

Jesus, my son — I pray it is true! Come back to us as you promised, for I am Mary, your grieving mother, and I am a woman of the promise!

Series 3

Come, Follow Me

Nicodemus

(Nicodemus is standing and reading from a large scroll that he holds in both hands. Beside him are several other scrolls either in a stand or on a table. He is obviously a student of the scriptures. He is dressed in good, expensive clothing appropriate for a Pharisee. He looks up from the scroll to see the audience, rolls up the scroll, and sets it down. He addresses the audience.)

"You must be born again." With those words, Jesus of Nazareth changed my life ... *forever.*

When he first said it, I have to admit he caught me off guard. I didn't know what to make of it. I tried to picture myself curling up as small as I could and being born a second time. I imagined my mother lying there and the midwives delivering me, their eyes as big as plates, and they stammer for a minute as my mother asks if it's a boy or a girl, and they say, "It's a ... *man!*" They try to hold me upside down and spank me as is done with newborns, but it takes five of them to pick me up before dropping me. Then they try to wrap me in swaddling cloths, but it takes all the sheets in the house to cover me. Finally, they present me to my mother, but not until first giving me a shave. Born again? How, indeed?

On the other hand I wondered, "Why?" Why would I even *want* to be born a second time? After all, I thought I had turned out pretty good the first time! I, Nicodemus, am wealthy, a respected Pharisee and the son of a Pharisee, an accomplished student of the law and the prophets, and a teacher of God's word, as well. Also, recently, with my appointment to the Sanhedrin, the supreme ruling council of my religion, I had arrived at a position in life many coveted, but few achieved. Be born again and have to start all over? Why would I want to?

So, testing Jesus, I objected and asked, "How can anyone be born after having grown old? Can one enter a second time into the mother's womb and be born?" My objection was obvious, but I wanted to hear how Jesus would answer, since he was certainly talking about something else.

Jesus answered me, "Very truly, I tell you, no one can enter the kingdom of God without being born of water and Spirit. What is born of the flesh is flesh, and what is born of the Spirit is spirit. The wind blows where it chooses, and you hear the sound of it, but you do not know where it comes from or where it goes. So it is with everyone who is born of the Spirit."

Now I really was puzzled, so I asked, "How can these things be?"

Jesus said, "Are you a teacher of Israel, and yet you do not understand these things? Very truly, I tell you, we speak of what we know and testify to what we have seen; yet you do not receive our testimony. If I have told you about earthly things and you do not believe, how can you believe if I tell you about heavenly things?"

Jesus' words stung me like a honeybee from the hives of Naphthali. To imply (no, to *proclaim!*) that I didn't know about the Spirit of God was a challenge to my education and position. I had come to Jesus to judge for myself what he was teaching, and instead he judged me and found me deficient! As I left Jesus that night and returned to my home, I was both disturbed and intrigued by what he had said. How could I be born of the Spirit?

I should have known something like this would happen. Other Pharisees had reported back to the Sanhedrin about their encounters with Jesus. In every case, they were upset because they had tried to catch Jesus in some trap, only to get caught themselves. One of my fellow Pharisees had asked Jesus if it is lawful to pay taxes to Caesar (a sore subject with us!) only to have Jesus point out the face of the Roman emperor on the coin and say, "Then give to the emperor the things that are the emperor's, and to God the things that are God's." Another time, they accused Jesus of healing on the sabbath, only to have him remind them that the law allowed a person to rescue an animal from a well on the sabbath, and that a human life was more important than an animal's. When I heard such stories I found myself amused, and even secretly cheering for Jesus and the way he cut through the pompous attitudes and hypocrisy of my fellow Pharisees.

The other seventy members of the Sanhedrin had already made up their minds that they did not approve of Jesus at all. Some were talking among themselves, first just whispers, then louder, that something must be done about Jesus before everyone started following him. The only other member who seemed somewhat sympathetic to Jesus was a man named Joseph, who was from the town of Arimathea. He and I would sometimes quietly discuss some of the things Jesus was teaching, and we marveled with each other about the miracles that were being reported — had Jesus really healed a man born blind, cleansed people of leprosy, and raised a girl from the dead?

I decided I had to find out more about Jesus. I told myself I was just doing my duty, because as a member of the Sanhedrin, I was responsible for the religious life of the nation, and I had to know whether Jesus was a threat to our religion or to our national peace. We have had too many false messiahs stirring up the people and provoking the Romans' armed retaliation. Was Jesus another troublemaker?

But deep down, I knew I was going to see Jesus for more personal reasons, because for all my outward success as a wealthy and respected Pharisee, there was an emptiness inside of me, a troubled soul under the contented mask. I knew much *about* God but wondered if I actually *knew* God. God seemed so far off, yet Jesus was talking as if he knew him personally, even calling him Father. I wanted to know more, so I went. But, even so, I felt guilty about seeking out Jesus, so I went under cover of night. I certainly didn't want the Sanhedrin to know what I was doing.

Now I had seen and heard him, and found my spirit stirring in me with questions about God, about Jesus, and about the possibility of new life. "You must be born again!" What could that mean? I decided I needed to ask Jesus to explain what he meant, but soon after our first meeting, Jesus left the Jerusalem region and returned to Galilee. I continued on in my Sanhedrin duties, but as reports came to us about Jesus, my conviction that he was a prophet sent by God grew.

That fall, Jesus returned with his disciples to Jerusalem for the Feast of Tabernacles, and things came to a head. By now, the chief priests and Pharisees decided it was time to put an end to Jesus and his growing popularity, so they sent a detachment of temple soldiers to arrest him and throw him into prison. I was greatly troubled by this, but I joined the Sanhedrin in our council chambers and we waited for the prisoner to be brought in. We waited for what seemed like hours, when finally the doors opened and the temple guard marched in — but without Jesus. Our leaders stood up and asked the guard, "Why did you not arrest him?" The guards answered, "Never has anyone spoken like this!" Well, at that our rulers shouted angrily, "Surely you have not been deceived too, have you? None of *us* believes in him. Are you agreeing with that uneducated mob out there? Curses on them and *you* if you are!"

For my own good I should have kept quiet, but I had to speak up. I asked the council, "Our law does not judge people without first giving them a hearing to find out what they are doing, does it?" My question seemed reasonable, and I was only suggesting we obey our own law, but they jumped all over me and shouted, "Surely you are not also from Galilee, are you? Search and you will see that no prophet is to arise from Galilee." I became silent as the debate about Jesus raged on, afraid if I said anything else I might be arrested myself! Finally, with nothing accomplished, the council broke up and we all went home.

On the way out, Joseph of Arimathea caught up with me and thanked me for speaking up. We talked and both agreed that no one ever did speak the way Jesus does. I told him about Jesus' command to be born again, and Joseph confided in me that he was now one of Jesus' disciples and believed that Jesus is truly the Messiah. He asked me not to tell anyone because of his position on the Sanhedrin. We agreed that some day we would show our support for Jesus more openly. Not until the next Passover did we realize what our promise would mean.

For it was at the next Passover when Jesus of Nazareth was arrested, tried illegally in a secret trial in the middle of the night, condemned, and executed by order of the Roman governor. My friend, Joseph, and I were powerless to stop the events of that horrible day, but before the sunset we made our public stand as Jesus' followers. We went to Pilate and took Jesus' body from him and prepared it for burial. I went to the marketplace and bought 75 pounds of myrrh and aloes to anoint the body, while Joseph prepared the strips of cloth. We wrapped him and laid him in Joseph's own tomb near the crucifixion site, finishing before sunset as the law required.

When word of our merciful actions spread, the Sanhedrin's anger at us grew, until Joseph and I were forced to resign our posts. We were no longer welcome among our fellow Pharisees, and we lost much of our wealth as persecution arose against Jesus' followers. Our old life was changed, had ended in a way, but that was okay, because now we had been *born again* to new life as disciples of Jesus Christ. Now we are truly alive — in the Spirit as well as the flesh — as followers of a Savior who was not only crucified, but risen again. Now I understand what Jesus was talking about, and now I know the meaning of the words Jesus spoke to me that day when he said I must be born again. He said to come and follow him, and so I follow him now to eternal life.

Martha

(She walks in carrying a tray with cups and a loaf of bread, or a pitcher in both hands with a cloth draped over one arm. There is a table out front on which to set the tray or pitcher. She looks busy and a bit preoccupied with her tasks, so she doesn't see the people who have "come in" to her home. She adjusts the placement of the items on the table to make them appear "just right.")

There! That should do it ... Now everything is just about ready ... All I need now is to get the fish and I'm ready for company.... *(looks over hard to one side at a "window")* Now that the sun has set, they should be here any moment; I just hope they don't get here too early before I'm ready for them. If Mary had helped me get ready I'd be done by now! *(starts to turn and go back to get the fish, when she catches sight of the audience)*

Oh, you're here! Shalom! Welcome to our home. Early? Oh, no, you're right on time! You are always welcome here! Everything's just about ready, once I put the fish on the fire and get my brother and sister from whatever they're doing. Mary *could* be helping put this dinner on, but ever since the first time Jesus came and supped with us, she's had her mind on heavenly things. As for Lazarus, well, he's probably showing off his grave cloths again to someone new. Oh, yes, grave cloths! Hadn't you heard about what happened to him? No? Well, that's a whole story in itself! Here, have a seat around the table — *(points)* that's where Lazarus sits, there's Mary's place, and that's where Jesus reclined when he ate with us just last week. My seat? *(pauses)* Well, I don't really have one at the table — you see, I'll be serving and going back and forth to the kitchen — so don't worry about me.

(points) Help yourself to some olives and dates while I call Mary and Lazarus ... *(turns and belts out loudly)* Maaarrry! Laaazzzarrrusss! Time to eat! Our company's here! *(turns back to audience, smiling)* There, they've been called!

The first time Jesus came to our house here in Bethany, I eagerly invited him and his disciples to come and rest and share our supper. We had heard some amazing things about him and wanted to meet him ourselves, so with Mary and Lazarus' approval, I extended the invitation. We were afraid that with all the attention he's getting, he would have more important people to spend time with, but to our surprise, he said yes to our offer. Of course, inviting someone to dinner is easy; the real work begins when they accept. I set to work building the cook fires, then cooking, baking, cleaning, washing — everything it takes to host company. Much like this evening, yes? Only that time, I had Mary's help, at least for a while.

Jesus sat down, and we served the meal. As the disciples ate, Jesus talked to them and taught them about God. It sounded very interesting, but I was so busy I couldn't take time to stop and listen very well. In fact, I was so busy serving, I didn't notice that Mary had stopped working and was sitting near Jesus, at his feet, listening to his every word.

When I finally realized Mary wasn't helping anymore, I got upset. Upset at Mary, for leaving me with all the work, and even at Jesus for letting her get away with it. So I went up to him and interrupted him to say, "Lord, don't you care that my sister has left me to do the work by myself? Tell her to help me!" But Jesus just said to me, "Martha, Martha, you are worried and upset about many things, but only one thing is needed. Mary has chosen what is better, and it will not be taken away from her."

Jesus said that in such a kind way, I couldn't stay angry. There was truth in what he said because the things he talked about were more important than all the fussing about I was doing. I did want to hear him teach. But still, what I was doing *was* important; because without someone preparing the food and serving it, everyone would have gone hungry. Should I also have left the work undone because of Jesus, or should I have continued to work *for* Jesus? I chose to continue working, because Jesus and his disciples needed to be fed.

The second time Jesus came to our house was quite different. It began in tragedy and turned into something incredible, something ... well, you judge for yourself. Our friendship with Jesus had grown since his first visit to us. Our brother, Lazarus, became especially devoted to him, and Mary, of course, talked about the kingdom of God every day, saying that Jesus himself could be the Messiah we have long waited for. Even I became more and more convinced that he was the anointed one of God. But Jesus left Bethany and took his disciples across the Jordan and back to Galilee, where large crowds gathered to hear him and be healed by his miracles.

Suddenly, one day, Lazarus took deathly ill. He couldn't get out of bed or even talk. He just lay there with a high fever. Mary and I did what we could for him, but all the traditional remedies had no effect on him. We called a physician to come and help, but Lazarus just got worse. Mary and I realized our brother could die, so we sent word by a messenger to Jesus, pleading with him to return to Bethany to heal Lazarus. Our message said, "Lord, the one you love is sick."

We prayed and we waited; the days passed by and Lazarus worsened, but still Jesus didn't come. Finally, one evening, it was over. Lazarus died, and Mary and I wept bitterly for him. Why hadn't Jesus come? Didn't he get our message? Didn't he truly love us and want Lazarus to live? Now, it was too late, so we buried our brother in a rocky tomb that had a large stone across its entrance, and we mourned his death, surrounded by many neighbors from Bethany and Jerusalem who tried to console us in our loss. The days passed.

On the fourth day after Lazarus' burial, a runner arrived at our house saying he had seen Jesus and his disciples on the road just outside of town, headed our way. I dropped what I was doing and, leaving Mary behind, I ran out the door and up the road. Soon, I found him. I told him, "Lord, if you had been here, my brother would not have died. But I know that even now God will give you whatever you ask." Jesus answered me, "Your brother will rise again." I replied, "I know he will rise again in the resurrection at the last day," for truly, I do believe what Jesus taught us about the resurrection to eternal life.

Then Jesus said these amazing words: "I am the resurrection and the life. He who believes in me will live, even though he dies, and whoever lives and believes in me will never die. Do you believe this?" I answered now, without any hesitation or doubt, "Yes,

Lord; I believe that you are the Christ, the Son of God, who was to come into the world." Then I ran back and told Mary that Jesus was asking for her. She went and talked to him as Jesus reached the village.

What happened next was beyond description — the most incredible and wonderful thing I have ever seen. Jesus wept; then went up to the tomb where our brother's lifeless body lay shrouded in linen. He commanded that the stone be rolled away. I warned him that we shouldn't do that because after four days in the tomb, the stench of death would be terrible. But we obeyed him, and then he spoke loudly, with authority in his voice, "Lazarus, come out!"

You can imagine our shock when just seconds later, out walked Lazarus! Alive! Still bound hand and food with bandages, and his face wrapped with a cloth. At Jesus' command, we took off his grave cloths, and there he stood, alive and healed!

This has certainly created a stir, as people come now to see Lazarus and hear his testimony about being raised from the dead. He shows off his cloths and jokes about getting a refund on the purchase of the cloth, but if you ask him what it was like to be dead for four days, all he says is, "That's for me to know and for you to find out!" Isn't that like a pesky little brother! But he has powerful testimony about what Jesus did for him, so much so that many are coming to believe with us that Jesus is the Savior sent from God.

Jesus stayed with us and dined once more at this table, just last week, but now he's gone into Jerusalem to prepare for the coming Passover feast. We offered to host him here again, but he said the hour has come for him to be glorified, and it must be in Jerusalem.

I would have liked to follow him into the city. I heard a cheering crowd greeted him with palm branches when he did, but I have work to do here. That's the way I will follow him, to do what I do well for him and for his kingdom. If I am a good cook, then I will feed those who preach in his name. If I wash clothing, I will clean the robes his disciples wear. And if I manage a household, I will do so well and save money to support Jesus and his work. Not all of his followers can be preachers — some have to do some real work, too!

(suddenly remembers the fish) Speaking of work, I almost forgot about the fish I'm cooking for your dinner! If I don't get it on the fire right away, it'll start smelling like *it's* been in the grave for four days. So just relax for now and eat some more olives, but if my sister, Mary, ever shows up, tell her that Martha has something for her to do in the kitchen! *(hurriedly exits)*

Judas

(He hurries along the road, clutching a bag full of coins, looking determined, but feeling a combination of anger and guilt as he encounters the audience.)

"Come, follow me!" Jesus said. "Leave everything and follow me!" he said.

(stops and turns to audience) That's easy enough for him to say; not so easy to do! Follow him where? At what cost? And what have I gotten out of following him? Not much, I can tell you that!

It's like a lot of what Jesus says. His words sound good and the crowds love to hear them, and maybe in the heavenly kingdom they could work. But not in the real world, not in a harsh land suffering under the Roman yoke. Turn the other cheek? Walk an extra mile? Give someone your cloak if you have two? Sounds good, but you'll just be taken advantage of. What if the other guy doesn't believe in Jesus? He'll take what you give him and just keep it for himself, and then come back for more because he figures you're an easy touch. And I can assure you, the Romans won't pack up and leave this country if we love our enemies as Jesus taught. If we love them too much, they'll like it here and want to stay!

"Come, follow me!" Jesus said.

Well, I did follow him! From Cana to the Transjordan, from the Sea of Galilee to the Dead Sea, through godforsaken Samaria to Judea, from Nazareth to Jerusalem. I followed him for almost three years now, wherever he went, but look where it's gotten me: nowhere! That's where! I'm no better off now than I was three years ago when he first told me to follow him.

I don't know why he even called me to be one of his disciples that day — there were plenty of other guys to choose from who would have given anything to follow him. I was in the synagogue that day, listening to Jesus teach, and like everyone else, I was impressed. After the service dismissed, Jesus looked at me, and walked right up to me and said to follow him, that I had a special place among his disciples, and had something important to do. I have no idea what he meant by that now, but when I first heard him say that, it sounded exciting! Here was Jesus, the teacher everyone was talking about, saying he wanted me!

It's not like he asked everyone to join his inner circle of disciples; he kept it small on purpose. The twelve he called us, just like the twelve tribes of Israel. He didn't take volunteers. To each of us he said, "You have not chosen me, I have chosen you!" which is pretty heady to hear. Can you imagine how I felt when he told me that? All those people who were clamoring to be seen with Jesus, and he chose me. Of *course* I left my job — sold it to my partner at cost — and took to the road as part of Jesus' team.

"Come, follow me!" Jesus said.

I saw a chance to get ahead in the world, to be respected and honored, and taken care of without a lot of backbreaking work. If Jesus should turn out to be the Messiah, then I was in on the ground level, and he would certainly reward me with a high position in his new government, maybe minister of the treasury.

So I followed. Right away, I took on the disciples' money purse since the only other disciples who had handled money before was Matthew. Since he had been a tax collector, well I didn't think we should trust him that much, even though Jesus had chosen him, too. People would give us a coin here or there so we could buy food, and I handled all the payments with those donations. Although we always seemed to have enough to live on, the treasury never seemed to grow. Jesus never seemed concerned about it. He just taught us to pray for our daily bread. I would have liked to have a few extra days' money in reserve, you never know when you might need it.

The truth is, if Jesus had wanted to, we could all have become very wealthy, indeed. All he had to do was charge people for those miraculous healings he was already doing! Physicians make a good living off their remedies and poultices — and they're not nearly as effective as Jesus. How much do you think people would pay to be able to see again? To walk again, to have their hearing restored, or to be free of leprosy? How much would that man, Jairus, have paid Jesus to bring his daughter back to life? Plenty, that's how much.

That guy was loaded, the ruler of his synagogue, but Jesus did it for free! It was frustrating for me to see Jesus miss golden opportunities to earn some serious gold.

Once, I thought he was finally getting it, when a rich, young ruler came to Jesus and asked what he had to do to inherit eternal life. When Jesus told him to get rid of his wealth, I got excited, because here was a chance for us to help the man by taking his wealth off his hands for him! But Jesus didn't ask for the money. He told the ruler to give it to the poor. Can you imagine that? What do you call *us* — wealthy? After that, I gave up on our little band growing rich and started to use some of the coins from our purse for some of my *personal* needs.

"Come, follow me!" Jesus said.

But he didn't go anywhere! Sure, from one dusty little village to another, up a hill, or back and forth across the Sea of Galilee. Nowhere important until now, when we arrived here in Jerusalem. Even now, he's not taking advantage of our being here to gain supporters. When we arrived in town on Sunday, a huge crowd met us along the road and cheered Jesus. They laid palm branches at his donkey's feet and shouted, "Hosanna!" which means, "Save us now!" What an opportunity to finally gather an army to take over and rule this place, but what did Jesus do? He went to the temple and proceeded to anger the very religious leaders whose help he needed, and his chance to seize power has all but evaporated like a mirage in the Negev desert.

"Come, follow me!" Jesus said.

You can follow Jesus if you want, but be warned — the road isn't easy. There will be sacrifices, and you'll be led places you may not want to go. You won't have the money or life of comfort we all want, and you may find people looking down on you. You may find yourself persecuted and hunted.

As for me ... I have followed Jesus this far, but no farther. If I stay with him, at best I'll be eating dusty roads for years to come; at worst, Jesus will get arrested and I'll go to prison with him. I had to do something to protect myself and look after my own interests, so I took matters into my own hands. *(holds up bag of coins)*

My hands like the feel of my future. *(hefts the bag a couple times)* Thanks to the generosity of the chief priests and a little arrangement between them and me; well, let's just say that my future is looking as bright as thirty pieces of polished silver.

So go ahead and follow Jesus, and I'll follow my own path. Then we'll see who's got the better future! *(exits, smirking)*

Mary Magdalene

(She hurries down the aisle toward the front of the church. She begins calling out as she comes down the aisle, turning to each side and entreating the audience. She is visibly upset and that comes through in her voice)

Help! Oh, please, help me! They have arrested him and taken him away, and I don't know where he is. Have you seen him? Help me find him, please!

(spoken in front of church, facing audience) Who? Jesus, of course! The master! They have taken him away! *(catches her breath)* He was at the Passover supper tonight with his disciples, and then they went out to the Garden of Gethsemane. I was with the other women here in Jerusalem when Philip came bursting into the house to tell us all is lost! He said that soldiers sent by the high priests arrived in the garden while the disciples slept. They found Jesus and arrested him! And unbelievably, one of Jesus' own disciples, Judas, led the soldiers there and even showed them which one was Jesus! How could he do that? None of this makes any sense! I mean, why would anyone betray Jesus, or arrest him? He's no criminal!

(thoughtfully) I mean, has there ever been a man like Jesus? Has there ever been anyone so unselfish, so caring about other people as Jesus? Has there ever been anyone so humble? Truth be known, I have never, ever seen anyone like him before!

Jesus has shown compassion to men and women alike, been friend to the friendless, loved the unlovable, healed diseases, and comforted those who mourned, not just with words, but by raising the dead! How could anyone, especially one of his closest followers, turn against Jesus, when they've been with Jesus for years and know just how good a man he is?

Most men seek honor and power. They struggle against each other to control and dominate, to climb to the top over all the others. *(looks disgusted and shakes her head)* I have even seen that among the twelve disciples, as they sometimes argue as to which of them is the greatest!

But Jesus is ... different. Jesus acts as if he already has power and honor, so he doesn't have to strive for it. Instead, he is willing to share it with everyone else. He taught us not to lord it over each other but to serve each other in humility. As for himself, Jesus told us that he did not come into the world to be served but to serve.

If we had needed any example of that, he showed us tonight. We had no sooner settled in and begun the Passover supper, when Jesus took off his outer cloak, wrapped a towel around his waist, and took a basin of water around to each of the disciples. He then began to wash their feet. *(smiles as she remembers)* You should have seen the looks on their faces! At first they protested, because he is our master and masters don't wash their followers' feet! That's normally the job of a servant or even a slave, certainly not the job of an honored rabbi! But Jesus replied, "Now that I, your Lord and teacher, have washed your feet, you also should wash one another's feet." He showed by his own humility how we are to treat each other.

Jesus is also unselfish. With all his miraculous powers, he could make lots of money if he wanted to. You've seen those street magicians, haven't you? They earn a few coins doing tricks or claiming to read minds. Some are quite entertaining, and others seem to actually have some special abilities. Well, can you imagine how much money Jesus could make if he set up shop somewhere and charged people for his miracles? Ten shekels for a healed foot, 100 for a new eye, five for a loaf of bread and you bring the stone! How many denarii to raise your son or daughter from the dead? Why, he could name his price for that!

But Jesus heals and feeds and raises the dead — for free! All he wants is their faith in him and in the heavenly Father. It takes a truly good man to give himself to others, and not let his power or popularity go to his head!

There's something else I really appreciate about our Lord Jesus, and that's the way he treats women. As you know, this is a rough time and place for women to live and prosper. In our country, women don't own property. We're not allowed to testify in court against a man. Our husbands can divorce us with a slip of paper and no good reason or compensation. If a man and woman are caught in adultery, guess which one gets punished! It's almost as if we are just property to be owned at a man's whim.

But Jesus treats us differently, with honor and respect. Once, Jesus and the disciples were traveling through Samaria when Jesus sat to rest near a village well. A woman from the village came to Jesus, and he spoke to her! What's so big about that? Just that men don't speak to strange women in public! Especially a foreigner! Then, he asked her for water, which could have made him "unclean," but he did so, and treated her kindly in order to teach her about God's forgiveness.

Another time, he took sympathy on a woman who was going to be stoned for adultery. Jesus told her to stop sinning, of course, and he sent her away unharmed after shaming her captors into not casting their stones at her.

That's just one reason a group of us women follow Jesus and the twelve, to serve them and help where we can, and to listen and learn from Jesus. We have found the Messiah, and we know that he cares about women as well as men, and about our relationship to God. We love Jesus and adore him. But unlike what some other men might do in his position, he has never taken advantage of our love for him by trying to do anything sinful. His love is pure and unselfish.

Yes, we follow Jesus willingly. But for me, I have another, very personal reason to follow him, for he set me free *(slowly)* from the power of *evil* itself! I don't really like to talk about the time before I knew Jesus because I was so miserable then, but you need to know why I am so grateful to Jesus, and why I cannot understand how anyone could have betrayed him!

You see, until Jesus set me free, I had been afflicted by seven unclean spirits — demons — who had come upon me to torment me and drive me crazy. I don't know when or how they all came to me; and until Jesus drove them out, I didn't even know for sure how many there were. All I know is that for years I had been their prisoner.

Unless you've been afflicted, you don't really know what it's like to have evil as your constant companion. They were always talking to me, telling me to do things I knew were against God's commandments. Even though I refused to do some of those things, the demons would tell me I was a horrible sinner, that God hated me, and only they could help me! At times they hurt me directly, and other times they tried to make me hurt myself. They told me to cut myself or to throw myself in the path of Roman soldiers as they galloped by on their horses. But I refused, crying out to God to help me and save me from those awful creatures.

Then Jesus came into my life. The day I met Jesus, I was under an especially powerful attack. I lay on the ground, crying and shaking, when Jesus strode right through the crowd that was watching me. I thought, "Great! Someone new to pity me!" Instead of looking helplessly at me or pitying me, Jesus spoke in a powerful, commanding voice right to the demons! He ordered them to come out of me, and when they tried to argue and defy him, he shut them up. Then came the most wonderful feeling of *freedom*, as one by one the demons left me. For the first time in years, I was clean and free — and I wept my joy and thanksgiving to Jesus.

I have followed him since that day, and I will follow him for the rest of my life. That's the way it must be, for in Jesus, I have found truth. In Jesus, I have found a good man, a humble man, one who sees past the social position of men and women to know and love them. In Jesus, I have found the greatest man who ever lived ... and more than a man. For in Jesus, I have found the Son of God, who defeated the powers of evil with his own power and authority.

(realization of Jesus' arrest hits her again) And now, I'm afraid I've lost him as well! Come, help me find him, wherever they've taken him — we'll speak to his captors and tell them how good a man Jesus is. We'll tell them there's been a mistake; they'll listen to us, and surely, they'll let him go! *(exits hurriedly as she continues to search for Jesus)*

Peter

(There is a table up front with a quill, inkstand, and parchment on it. Peter paces back and forth anxiously, lost in thought, but suddenly looks up a couple times toward the audience as if waiting for someone to arrive. Finally he sees the expected person arrive, imaginary or played by a nonspeaking actor, and motions eagerly for him to come in. Peter is dressed plainly in "prison garb.")

Oh, there you are! You are the scribe I asked for, aren't you? *(pauses for "answer")* Good! I've been waiting for you and was afraid you might be delayed! Please, take a seat and let's get started, because *(thoughtfully)* I don't have much time, and I want to get this letter written. *(points)* There is parchment ... there is ink ... when you are ready, I'll begin.

*(Most of what follows is spoken as if dictating to the scribe, appearing in **bold** letters, with an occasional comment to the scribe personally.)*

Simon Peter, an apostle of Jesus Christ, to God's elect who are scattered throughout the churches of Asia Minor; praise be to the God and Father of our Lord Jesus Christ!

(to the scribe) Am I going too fast? No? That's good. *(goes back to dictating the letter)*

I have received your many recent epistles that contain such gracious prayers for my well-being, and such wonderful news about how your churches have grown since I last saw you. I am filled with joy to hear how the gospel is advancing, and thank you for making such efforts to write and send me your letters. They have brought me great encouragement and peace. I also read how some of you have come under persecution for your beliefs, that some were beaten by hostile crowds, some driven from your homes, and others arrested and thrown into prison.

(to the scribe) You look surprised, but I'm not the only one who has been arrested for faith in Jesus Christ. We have been arrested for many things. As a nonbeliever, you may have heard some of the charges made against us Christians: Have you heard that we disturb the peace? That we are atheists because we do not worship

all the Roman gods? That we hurt the economy because we don't buy silver and gold idols? That we are cannibals because we gather to eat the body and drink the blood of our leader? *(smiles)* Oh, don't worry ... I'm not hungry right now! Besides, we eat bread and drink wine, which our Lord told us was his body and blood, given and shed for our forgiveness, so you can relax. Let me continue. *(goes back to dictating the letter)*

Believe me when I say that I understand your suffering, for I have received such treatment many times myself. But now some of you are asking about the cost you must pay to follow Jesus. You want to know where it will lead and if it is worth it. While I don't know what will happen to each and every one of you in the short term, I can assure you that what the Lord has in store for your eternal future is well worth anything that may happen to you now.

When our Lord, Jesus, calls us and says, "Come, follow me," we have only one true and proper response, and that is to drop everything and follow him, wherever he may lead. I have tried to do this in my own life, and I can tell you I do not regret where it has taken me. The first time I heard Jesus' call was on the shores of the Sea of Galilee, when he came and told me to drop my fishing nets and follow him, for he would make me a fisher of men.

(to the scribe) Does that sound strange to you? You don't have to write all this down, but, yes, I was a fisherman ... and a good one at that! The fish of the Galilean Sea quivered whenever my boat drew close to them. Why, you could even hear their little scales rattling in fear! Many of their brothers and sisters had already met my net and gone on to grace the tables of Bethsaida, so they knew their time would be soon! But one night, my partners and I had spent the entire night fishing without a single catch. In the morning, we came back to shore and were cleaning our nets when we saw Jesus standing on the shore, teaching a crowd of people. When he saw us, he climbed in our boat and had us push out from shore so he had room to better speak to the crowd. Then, he told us to push out to even deeper water and to let out our nets one more time. His words made no sense to me, but I did as he said. We cast

out our nets *(excitedly)* and were overwhelmed with all the fish we caught! So many fish, the nets were in danger of tearing! I called our partners to join us in their boat and soon both boats were almost sinking from the catch —☐it was so big!And I thought *I* was a great fisherman! Jesus could work for me any time!

But that's not what Jesus wanted. He wanted my brother, Andrew, and me and our partners, James and John, to work for him, catching something worth far more than fish. He wanted us to catch people for God's kingdom. So we returned to shore, left our nets, and followed Jesus. We never looked back. It may be hard for you to believe or understand, since you don't know him, but Jesus is not just any teacher or religious leader. He is the Christ, the Son of the living God.

I remember the first time I realized that and said it out loud. The other disciples and I were with Jesus one day when he asked us who people said he was. We told him the various things we had heard: Some said he was John the Baptist, others that he was the prophet Elijah.

Then Jesus looked directly at us — he had a way of doing that, of looking directly into your soul as if he could see every thought you ever had — and asked us, "Who do *you* say that I am?" That was when I realized in my heart that I knew who he was, and the words blurted out of my mouth with no hesitation: "You are the Christ, the Son of the living God." Jesus accepted what I professed and said God had revealed it to me.

Because Jesus is the Son of God — and God's chosen Savior of the world — how could I *not* follow him? *(pauses)* Okay, now where was I in my letter? *(pauses to hear the answer)* Okay.

And so, I answered Jesus' call, and followed him wherever he went, throughout Galilee and Judea and even Samaria, as he taught the crowds about the kingdom of God, healed the sick, cast out demons, and performed many powerful miracles. He sometimes sent us disciples out on short trips to neighboring towns where we, too, healed many people.

(to the scribe) Oh, yes! Miracles! If I had remained a fisher of fish, I would have missed out on the many incredible miracles that Jesus performed. By following Christ I witnessed God's power at

work in so many amazing ways. I saw Jesus calm storms, walk on water, heal the sick, and even raise the dead! And speaking of miracles, you should have been there when three of us disciples witnessed Jesus when he revealed his heavenly glory by shining like the sun! You don't believe me, do you? Well, pick up your quill and write this down, anyway.

I followed Jesus onto the mountain where he was transfigured, his face and clothing shining like the sun. I followed Jesus to Jerusalem where we had a last Passover supper together. I followed him to the garden of Gethsemane where they arrested him.

(to the scribe) Did I always follow him? No, I tried, and even followed him as he was taken to the high priest's house for trial that night, but to my shame I was so afraid, that when people asked me if I was one of his disciples, I denied I even knew him! Though I was guilty as sin, he forgave me and told me to care for his followers as a shepherd does for his sheep. His love for us is amazing! *(quickly)* Go on, don't stop writing; I have to finish this letter.

As you know, after Jesus was crucified, I at first thought my days of following him were over, that all our hopes and dreams had been destroyed with him. But then, three days later, came the wonderful news that Jesus' tomb was empty and that he had risen from the dead! We were all overjoyed, as we saw and touched him for ourselves, and learned from him that everything had happened to fulfill God's purpose. For Jesus Christ had to die as the final sacrifice for sin, so that we might be forgiven and have eternal life.

(to the scribe) You see, that's what our faith is all about — that God sent his own Son into the world to take our sins with him onto the cross. Then he rose again, to show that God has accepted his sacrifice. By doing so, he showed that we, too, will be raised on the last day. Yes, he died for you, too ... for Romans as well as for Jews. You, too, can have the eternal life that he promised to us. Christ calls you to follow him. Recognize your sinfulness before God, repent and be baptized in Jesus' name. He will forgive you and receive you into his kingdom. I would tell you more now, but the guards are coming for me — I can hear the sounds of their

armor even now! When you deliver this letter, talk to the Christian brothers and sisters who receive it; they will welcome you with open arms and tell you more. But for now, write quickly; I must finish this letter!

Our Lord Jesus told us to take up our crosses and follow him; now I have the privilege of doing so in reality. But you need not grieve for me — you should not. Because though I follow Jesus to the cross, and will no longer see you in this world, I know that I will also follow Jesus to the resurrection. And so will you, if you remain in him and follow him where he takes you. Peace to all of you who are in Christ. To him be glory both now and forever! Amen.

(A guard comes forward, unlocks the gate, and begins to escort him away.)

(to the scribe) And to you, my good scribe, deliver my letter, and thank you for helping me to speak once more of our precious Lord Jesus, who calls us and you, saying, "Come, follow me!" *(guard escorts Peter away to his cross)*

www.ingramcontent.com/pod-product-compliance
Lightning Source LLC
Chambersburg PA
CBHW060140050426
42448CB00010B/2230